Late Of This Address

LATE OF THIS

by Ian Hornby

CHARACTERS
Vicky Maddocks
Rick Maddocks
Jessica
Ronald
Charlotte Swift

The action passes in the living room of a small country cottage. The play is set in the mid nineteen-eighties.

ACT I Scene 1 .... An evening in late summer
ACT I Scene 2 .... A few moments later
ACT II Scene 1 .... The following morning
ACT II Scene 2 .... A moment later
ACT II Scene 3 .... Evening the same day
ACT III .... The following morning

PRODUCTION NOTES

There are several instances where RICK and VICKY fall under the influence of JESSICA and RONNIE. It is vital that these trances are not overplayed. Unless specifically directed, RICK and VICKY are fully conscious and aware of what they are doing, but cannot find the will to resist. Care should be taken to avoid any impressions of "trances".

ACT I Scene 1

About seven-thirty one evening in late summer. The play is set in the living room of a small country cottage. The decoration is shabby, having been empty for the last fifteen years. There are cobwebs in abundance and evidence of damp shown

Late Of This Address   **ACT I Scene 1**

by peeling wallpaper and stains on the walls. Nevertheless, apart from the dust the layout of the furniture is as if the room had just been vacated. Up a few stairs R a door leads to a small entrance hall. L is the door to the rest of the cottage. There is a dusty old dresser above L and a small leaded window above R.

As the curtain rises the stage is empty. The room is gloomily lit by the light from the window. The door R is ajar. A key is heard in the lock and the door opens off R.

RICK: *(Off R)* Wait a minute, Mrs Maddocks. We've got to do this properly.

VICKY: *(Off R; excitedly)* Rick! Stop it! Put me down!

   (RICK appears through the door R carrying VICKY "over the threshold". RICK wears an ordinary inexpensive suit, shirt and tie. VICKY wears a smart but inexpensive dress.)

RICK: Here we are. Home at last.

VICKY: Will you put me down!?

   (RICK puts Vicky down. They survey the room. RICK tries the light switch several times, but nothing happens.)

VICKY: God, I'd forgotten how awful the place looks.

RICK: Now don't start that again. It's not so bad. Considering what we paid for it. I'll try and find the meter. *(He exits L.)*

VICKY: *(Running her finger through the dust on the dresser; calling)* Everything's so filthy. *(She walks slowly round the room.)*

RICK: *(Off L)* Ah!

   (There is the clunk of a switch off L and the room lights come on. RICK enters L wiping the dust from his hands and sleeves.)

VICKY: It'll take weeks to get this place in order.

RICK: *(Taking her in his arms)* But, darling, we've *got* weeks. We've got all the time in the world.

VICKY: I still think we should've stayed with Auntie Vera until we've got the place done up a bit.

RICK: Nonsense! Surely it's better that we're here. We can get the important places cleaned up first....

VICKY: *(Moving away)* The kitchen, bathroom, in here...

RICK: Not forgetting the bedroom...!

VICKY: *(Playful)* Behave!

RICK: *(Grabbing her round the waist)* Why should I? Apart from that weekend in Devon, when we were both still reeling from the wedding, I've behaved like a monk. We've been under the eagle eye of Auntie Vera ever since. I'm fed up of behaving. Give us a kiss!

VICKY: *(Playfully evading him)* No! Not until we've at least cleaned up a bit. I

Late Of This Address   **ACT I Scene 1**

feel filthy already. This furniture makes my flesh creep.

RICK: *(Moving to the settee; sarcastic)* How dare you!? You're talking about the new Maddocks family heirlooms here!

(He pats the back of the settee. Dust flies up, making him cough.)

VICKY: It'll all have to go.

RICK: We'll have to use some of it. We can't exactly afford to refit the whole house, can we?

VICKY: But it's disgusting, the lot of it. Why we had to buy it I'll never know.

RICK: It came with the house. You might be surprised, there could be some valuable antiques here.

VICKY: Firewood, the lot of it.... If it's not too damp to catch light!

RICK: We'll have to make the best of it, then buy new as and when we can afford it. At least we've got a new bed.

VICKY: Yes... I can tell the way *your* mind works!

RICK: *(With an enthusiastic hand-clap)* Right! Where do we start?

VICKY: Where indeed? You take the cases upstairs while I see if I can get the boiler lit. I'll need gallons of hot water and a year's supply of Flash to get through this lot.

RICK: Right. *(Indicating off L)* The boiler's through there.

VICKY: *(Moving to the door L and opening it)* I know where it is. Roughly. I just hope I don't get lost in all the cobwebs. If I don't come back in ten minutes send in a search party. *(She exits L. Off L)* Ugh! Oh, my God! It's disgusting out here.

(RICK smiles to himself, turns and exits R. He returns a few moments later carrying two old suitcases. He crosses to the door L and exits.)

RICK: *(Off L)* Found it?

VICKY: What?

RICK: The boiler... Have you found it?

VICKY: *(Off L)* Oh, yes, I found it.... At least I *think* it's a boiler.

RICK: Don't blow us up, will you?

(The sounds of footsteps ascending stairs, then sounds of VICKY cursing are heard off L.)

VICKY: *(Calling from off L)* It doesn't look as if it's been touched for centuries.

(The sounds of footsteps descending stairs is heard off L.)

RICK: What?

VICKY: *(Entering L, her hands and face blackened with dirt)* That boiler. It's all rusted up. I could hardly get the valve to move.

RICK: Did it light?

Late Of This Address ACT I Scene 1

VICKY: No... No chance. We'll have to get someone in. *(She notices her hands.)* God, I'm filthy!
RICK: I'll have a look at it later.
VICKY: You can look as long as you want. You won't get it lit.
RICK: You're talking to "Repair Man Extraordinaire", here!
VICKY: Maybe... But even if "Repair Man Extraordinaire" *does* manage to shift the valve, he won't get it going if he hasn't got any matches, will he?
RICK: Ah..! No matches. That *could* be a problem.
VICKY: We must have been mad buying this place.
RICK: Now, Vicky..., don't start all that again.
VICKY: D'you think we'll *ever* get it fixed up?
RICK: *(Putting his arms around her)* Of course we will. Come on, cheer up. *(RICK kisses Vicky and during the kiss she puts her hands to his face, leaving dirty marks. They break.)*
VICKY: It's falling to bits.
RICK: A couple of days and you won't recognise the place. *(Pulling her to him)* Come on, how about another kiss?
VICKY: *(Seeing the marks on his face)* You're filthy!
RICK: I only wanted a kiss!
VICKY: I meant your face! *(She rubs off the marks from his face with her hands, then kisses him lightly.)*
RICK: Come on, let's get started. *(He starts to tidy up.)*
VICKY: *(Looking round the room; gloomy)* We must have been mad.
RICK: You already said that.
VICKY: *Normal* couples buy nice new semis.
RICK: *(Stopping working)* Vicky... We've been through all this. We can't *afford* a nice new semi. Now come on....
VICKY: Even waiting for a council house would've been better than this.
RICK: What *is* the matter with you?
VICKY: How long did the estate agent say this house has been empty?
RICK: About twenty years. Why?
VICKY: Exactly.
RICK: *(Puzzled)* What?
VICKY: "*Why...?*" That's what I'd like to know. *Why* has it been empty all that time?
RICK: *I* don't know.
VICKY: Perhaps we should have asked.
RICK: It's a bit late for second thoughts now.

4

VICKY: I knew it was too good to be true. I know the place is run down and damp *now*, but it can't have been this bad for twenty years, can it?

RICK: No, but....

VICKY: So why was it going so cheap?

RICK: What does it matter? We managed to get it, and....

VICKY: Because nobody else *wanted* it, that's why.

RICK: You don't know that.

VICKY: Then why didn't somebody buy it? Answer me that. You said yourself how cheap it was.

RICK: Well, it's a bit far from the shops and schools and so on....

VICKY: Not if you've got a car.

RICK: That sort of thing puts a lot of people off.

VICKY: It didn't put *us* off.

RICK: No, I know, but... *(Pause)* What is it, Vicky? You were happy enough when we looked round it, and happy enough when we bought it, so why the sudden change of heart?

VICKY: *(Looking uneasily around the room)* I don't know... It's just... just a feeling.

RICK: A feeling...? What sort of feeling?

VICKY: I don't know... I can't explain it.

RICK: You're just tired after the journey. You'll be O.K. tomorrow.

VICKY: *(Unconvinced)* Maybe... The place just makes me shiver.

RICK: *(Trying to be brighter)* It wouldn't if you'd got the boiler going.

VICKY: It's not the cold... It's just... *(She trails off.)*

RICK: You didn't get the shivers when we looked round. Or, at least, if you did you didn't say so.

VICKY: It was different... The place seems.... *(She cannot find a better word.)* different.

RICK: *(Looking round)* Looks exactly the same to me. How is it different?

VICKY: *(Frustrated by not understanding her own fears)* I.. don't.. know.... Only that it *is*. I never realised before how dark the rooms are.

RICK: Dark...? It's not dark.... *(Glancing at his watch)* Anyway, it's gone seven already. It gets dark quicker in the country.

VICKY: *(Suddenly, with a hint of desperation)* Let's leave, Rick.

RICK: *(Taken aback)* What!?

VICKY: *(Starting to panic)* Let's go. Now.., this minute.

RICK: Vicky! You're being ridiculous. This is our *home*.

VICKY: It's a house... It *isn't* a home.

Late Of This Address   ACT I Scene 1

RICK: It will be.... I promise. *Our* home.

VICKY: We could sell it again.

RICK: Sell it...!? Even if I wanted to... and I don't..., how could we? As you pointed out it's already been on the market for the last twenty years, so we're hardly likely to sell it again overnight.

VICKY: I don't care. I just want to leave. We can go back to Auntie Vera's.

(RICK is exasperated.)

VICKY: *(Pleading)* Please, Rick.

RICK: *(Getting annoyed)* This is stupid, Vicky. This is *our* house. It took ages to get a mortgage on it and for those blasted solicitors to get their act together and I'm *damned* if I'm going to just walk out of it because you're afraid of the dark!

VICKY: *(After a pause)* Don't you love me?

RICK: *(Still angry)* What the hell's *that* got to do with it!?

VICKY: If you love me, you'll take me away.... Now.

RICK: No! You're being totally irrational.

VICKY: *(Tearful)* I'm not! I hate it here.

RICK: *(Incredulous)* You *hate* it!? Not ten minutes ago you were sitting in the car planning what colour wallpaper you wanted! And now.... you hate it! *(He shakes his head in disbelief.)*

VICKY: *(Desperate)* It's different...!

RICK: *(Inflamed)* Give me one rational reason why you're doing this, Vicky. Just one!

VICKY: *(Near to tears)* I told you...!

RICK: *(Acidic)* You've told me nothing...! I've always looked on you as sensible and level-headed. In the ten minutes since we walked in here you've changed into a gibbering idiot. And the only reason you've managed to come up with is that it's getting dark and cold and you feel *uneasy*..! I've never seen this side of you before. And I can't say I like it.

VICKY: *(Reacting)* D'you think *I* do!?

RICK: Then pull yourself together and stop being so bloody stupid!

VICKY: *(Sobbing)* Please, Rick....

(RICK takes several moments to calm himself down. Eventually he goes to the sobbing Vicky and puts his arms round her.)

RICK: I'm sorry, darling. I didn't mean it.

(VICKY sobs into Rick's shoulder.)

VICKY: So am I.

RICK: Come and sit down and explain it all to me. *(He leads her to the settee and sits with her.)*

Late Of This Address   **ACT I Scene 1**

VICKY: *(Desperate)* I *can't* explain it. I don't know.

RICK: Just tell me what you feel... Anything.

VICKY: It's difficult to explain. I was alright when we first came in. The same in the kitchen, but when I came back in here I just felt.... *(She trails off and looks anxiously around the room.)*

RICK: What?

VICKY: "Cold" is the only word to describe it.

RICK: But I *told* you... It's getting late. And the place is damp... And these old houses have draughts.

VICKY: No...! You just don't understand, do you? It's not that sort of cold. There was no draught. The cold was sudden. I was O.K. one minute, then suddenly I felt this cold, sort of damp and clammy.

RICK: *(Taking her hands in his and trying to bring things back to normality)* Vicky... *(As if to a child; firmly)* There's nothing wrong with this house. You're used to a centrally-heated modern flat. This place has been empty for twenty years. No heat, no fresh air, nothing. It's *bound* to feel cold and clammy.

VICKY: *(Dubious)* But it wasn't just that...

RICK: And you were all excited and ready to move in, and... *(Looking round)* Just look at the place. Even *I'd* forgotten just how run down it is.

VICKY: Yes, I suppose so...

RICK: *(Trying to lift her spirits)* Let's get that boiler going and some heat on and you won't know the place.

VICKY: We haven't got any matches, remember?

RICK: Oh, no... Never mind. I spotted an off-licence in the village. You start cleaning up in here and I'll just drive down there and get some. I could get us some...

VICKY: *(Quickly; grasping his arm; afraid again)* No!

RICK: *(Surprised)* What!?

VICKY: I'm not staying here alone.

RICK: Vicky....! I'll only be five minutes.

VICKY: Please, Rick.

RICK: *(Calming)* Alright, alright. *I'll* start cleaning up and *you* get the matches.

VICKY: *(Uneasy)* We could both go.

RICK: What *are* you afraid of? Ghosts!?

VICKY: *(Looking nervously around again)* I... I don't know...

RICK: If we both go we'll *never* get unpacked. *(He pulls her up and propels her to the door R.)* Now off you go. Get some matches and a bottle of brandy, or something. Maybe it'll calm your nerves.

VICKY: Will you be O.K?

7

Late Of This Address   **ACT I Scene 1**

RICK: *(Pushing her out)* Go! If I meet and headless nuns I'll call "Ghostbusters"!
VICKY: Don't even joke about it.
RICK: Will you *go*!?
   (RICK puts his face forward for a kiss. VICKY kisses him, but her eyes are wide and scanning the room nervously.)
RICK: Wow..! That had all the passion of a wet lettuce.
VICKY: I'm sorry, Rick...
RICK: *(Pushing her out)* See you in five minutes.
   (They exit R. The front door is heard to open and close off R.)
RICK: *(Off R; calling)* Don't forget the brandy!
   (A car is heard to start and leave off R. After a few moments RICK enters R, bemused. He sets about clearing up the room picking up things from the floor, straightening the furniture and blowing dust off ledges. As he tidies the mantleshelf he knocks over an old statue and it smashes in the hearth.)
RICK: *(Picking up the pieces)* Damn! I quite liked that.
   (RICK takes the pieces off L. JESSICA enters R. She is dressed very smartly, at odds with the surroundings, but wears a very dated sixties-style short miniskirt and blouse. She looks around the room disapprovingly, noticing the broken statue. She moves up L. RICK enters facing down R so that he does not see Jessica. He moves R.)
JESSICA: *(Frosty)* Who the hell are you?
RICK: *(Whirling round, shocked)* My God! Don't do that! You gave me the fright of my life.
JESSICA: I repeat... Who *are* you?
RICK: I might ask you the same question.
JESSICA: *(Advancing)* Get out of my house at once!
RICK: What!?
JESSICA: You heard me!
RICK: *Your* house!? But this is *my* house.
JESSICA: Who *are* you?
RICK: *(Firmly)* I am Richard Maddocks, and this is *my* house!
JESSICA: You're not one of those squatters, are you?
RICK: No, I'm not, and I hardly think you're in any position to...
JESSICA: You'll have to leave.
RICK: Me!?
JESSICA: Now!
RICK: I can assure you I have no intention of leaving. Perhaps *you* had better leave.

Late Of This Address ACT I Scene 1

JESSICA: Impossible!
RICK: *(Pointing R)* There's the door.
JESSICA: You can't stay here.
RICK: Now look here, whatever your name is...
JESSICA: *(Threatening him)* You *can't stay*. This is *my* house.
RICK: This is ridiculous. I don't know what your game is, but...
JESSICA: I *don't* play games.
RICK: But whatever it is, I can assure you this is *my* house, bought and paid for. And I'm not leaving.
JESSICA: We'll see about that!
RICK: Yes, we will. I shall call the Police and see what they think.
JESSICA: We're not on the phone!
RICK: Then when my wife comes back I shall call them from the village.
JESSICA: At least that means you'll leave.
RICK: I don't believe this. You claim this is your house?
JESSICA: I don't *claim*... It *is* my house!
RICK: Then would you like to explain why I have the deeds registered with my building society, why I have the keys to the door, why the estate agent in the village....
JESSICA: That Eastwood woman?
RICK: Yes... Why?
JESSICA: Don't believe anything *she* says. She's been trying to sell this house for the last twenty years.
RICK: *(Taken aback) Trying* to sell it...? You mean it wasn't for sale?
JESSICA: No... I told you. It's mine.
RICK: But the solicitors... the searches. How d'you explain those?
JESSICA: *I* don't know. It's hardly *my* problem.
RICK: You've owned this house for twenty years?
JESSICA: Twenty-two.
RICK: But surely.... I mean.... You don't look old enough.
JESSICA: *(Dry)* I wear well.
RICK: *(Sitting)* This can't be happening.
JESSICA: *(After a pause; suddenly warmer)* Are you married?
RICK: What!?
JESSICA: I said "Are you married?"
RICK: What's that got to do with it?
JESSICA: *(Almost teasing)* Tell me.

Late Of This Address   ACT I Scene 1

RICK: Yes, I am as a matter of fact.... But I don't see....
JESSICA: Where is she?
RICK: Vicky?
JESSICA: Is that her name?
RICK: She's gone into the village.
JESSICA: I don't like it.
RICK: What?
JESSICA: Vicky. It's an awful name.
RICK: *(Defensive) I* happen to like it.
JESSICA: It's a child's name.
RICK: Look, I don't see what my wife's name has got to do with anything.... I want to know what...
JESSICA: How long will she be?
RICK: Only a few minutes. Why?
JESSICA: *(Advancing on him)* I thought we could get to know each other better.
RICK: *(Backing away)* Look, Miss....
JESSICA: *(Correcting him)* Mrs.
RICK: I really don't think that we... that you... I mean... *(Thinking fast)* What about your husband?
JESSICA: He's not here. He went away.
RICK: *(Still retreating)* Even so, my wife could be back at any minute, and...
JESSICA: Are you frightened of me?
RICK: *(Against the mantlepiece L; hoarse)* No, of course not, but...
JESSICA: *(Stroking his collar)* Most men are.
RICK: Are they?
JESSICA: Terrified. *(Stroking his hair)* I can't think why.... Can you?
(There are sounds of a car drawing up off R. JESSICA is distracted by it and RICK uses the opportunity to duck out of her clutches.)
RICK: *(Moving R)* That sounds like Vicky now. I'd better go and help her with the.... er.. matches. (He dashes off R.)
(JESSICA looks mildly annoyed. The front door is heard to open off R.)
RICK: *(Off R; calling)* Darling...! You're back at last!
(JESSICA goes unhurriedly to the window and looks out, grimaces and slowly exits L.)
VICKY: *(Off R)* What d'you mean "at last"? It's only just down the road! *(She enters R carrying a carrier bag from an off licence.)*
RICK: *(Entering R; about to explain who Jessica is)* This is.... *(He is surprised to find the room empty.)* Oh..!

10

VICKY: *(Puzzled)* What?

RICK: She was here a minute ago.

VICKY: *(Taking a small bottle of brandy and a box of matches from the carrier bag)* Who was?

RICK: This girl.... *(He trails off.)*

VICKY: What girl?

RICK: There was a girl here. She reckons *she* owns the house.

VICKY: She *what*!?

RICK: *(Moving to the door L)* What the hell's she up to now?

(RICK exits L, leaving the door ajar. VICKY looks round the room again and shivers. Rick can be heard opening doors, going upstairs, etc.)

RICK: *(Off L)* Hello.... Mrs... *(He realises he does not know her name.)* Hello... Where are you?

VICKY: *(Moving L; calling)* Rick... What *is* going on?

RICK: *(Entering L; puzzled)* She's not there.

VICKY: *(Losing patience)* Who isn't there?

RICK: *(Distracted)* I told you... This girl.

VICKY: For God's sake, Rick, will you tell me what on earth you're going on about!?

RICK: This girl... She came in, just after you left. She told me to get out of *her* house.

VICKY: *Her* house?

RICK: Yes.

VICKY: Didn't you tell her it was ours?

RICK: Yes, course I did, but she said she'd been living here for the last twenty-two years.

VICKY: That's ridiculous!

RICK: That's what *I* said.

VICKY: Who was she?

RICK: I don't know. She never said her name.... She was married, though.

VICKY: How d'you know?

RICK: I called her" Miss" and she corrected me to "Mrs".

VICKY: Was her husband with her?

RICK: No... She said he'd gone away. And the way she acted.... *(He trails off.)*

VICKY: Why? What did she do?

RICK: Well, one minute she was threatening to throw me out, and then all of a sudden she started coming on strong, like she fancied me.

VICKY: *(Unsure whether to be outraged or amused)* She what!?

Late Of This Address   ACT I Scene 1

RICK: It's just as well you came back when you did.

VICKY: And then she ran off?

RICK: She must have done. She's not in the house. Unless there's some secret room we don't know about.

VICKY: Hardly. With only four rooms in the place it'd be a bit hard to hide another. D'you think we should call the Police?

RICK: And tell them what? Trespass isn't a criminal offence, you know.. *(A pause.)* I wonder if it's possible... *(He trails off.)*

VICKY: What?

RICK: What if she's right? What if *we're* the trespassers?

VICKY: That's ridiculous! They did all those searches and things. And the Estate Agent...

RICK: She told me that Mrs Eastwood had been trying to sell the house for the past twenty years.

VICKY: So...? She told *us* that, too.

RICK: But this girl said it wasn't for sale. Maybe Mrs Eastwood.... And Mr Sharpe.... God, it doesn't bear thinking about.

VICKY: I can't believe an estate agent and a solicitor would put together some elaborate plot to sell us this dilapidated old place.

RICK: You read about these things.

VICKY: That's crazy! Anyway, who would you believe... an estate agent with several branches and a partner in a law firm or some cranky woman who turns up out of the blue, claims she owns *our* house, tries to seduce you and then runs off like a scared rabbit as soon as I come back?

RICK: *(Realising he is being foolish)* Alright. Point taken. *(A pause.)* It's just that she was so... believable.

VICKY: Most con artists are... I think we'd better report this to the Police, don't you?

RICK: *(Not fully convinced)* Well, yes, I suppose so.

VICKY: We *have* to, Rick. She may be dangerous.

RICK: Yes, I know, but.... Maybe we should check with Mrs Eastwood first. Just to be absolutely sure.

VICKY: I think we should phone the Police now. She can't have gone far. Maybe they could find her.

RICK: Out here? She could be anywhere. And I don't suppose there's a Police station in the village anyway. No, let's wait till morning.

VICKY: All right. If you think it's best.

RICK: One good thing, though.

VICKY: What?

Late Of This Address ACT I Scene 1

RICK: At least you've started calling it "our house" again. Ten minutes ago you wanted to leave.

VICKY: Yes, I'm sorry, darling. Maybe you were right - I was tired. The place just seemed so cold and intimidating.

RICK: And now?

VICKY: *(Calmly looking round)* No problem. I'm not cold any more.

(A key is heard in the door off R. The front door opens and closes off R.)

VICKY: *(Starting; hushed)* What's that?

RICK: *(Hushed)* Sounds like she's back.

(The door R opens slowly and CHARLOTTE enters. She is about sixty years old and wears a tweed skirt, a twin-set and brogue shoes. Since she is carrying several old small hard-backed books against her chest with one arm and her large handbag in the other hand she has a struggle opening the door. Because of this she backs into the room and does not see Rick and Vicky. She has a flash camera round her neck. Suddenly she sees them and starts, dropping her books.)

CHARLOTTE: *(Rather too shocked - she believes she is seeing ghosts)* Oh!

VICKY: *(To Rick)* Is this the one?

RICK: *Her*!? You're joking. I wouldn't want *her* to seduce me!

CHARLOTTE: *(Collecting herself)* Young man, I can assure you I have no intention of *seducing* you...

VICKY: Who are you?

CHARLOTTE: *(Excitedly)* I might ask *you* the same question. *(She raises her camera quickly and takes a flash photograph of them.)*

RICK: *(Annoyed)* What the hell d'you think you're doing?

VICKY: And how come you've got a key to our house?

CHARLOTTE: Oh, this *is* exciting! I've never actually *seen* you before. I hope the photograph comes out. D'you mind if I take some more?

RICK: Yes, we do! *(To Vicky)* This place is full of cranks.

(CHARLOTTE starts to pick up her books. One has fallen under the sideboard and she does not notice it.)

VICKY: Did the Estate Agent give you that key?

CHARLOTTE: No, I... *(She is beginning to realise that they are not the ghosts she thought they were.)* You... you arrived here tonight, did you?

RICK: Yes. About ten minutes ago. And ever since it's been like Euston Station. How many more people just come and go as they please in this place? It's more like a time-share than a home!

CHARLOTTE: Look, I'm sorry, I don't understand.... Are you trying to tell me you've *bought* this place?

Late Of This Address ACT I Scene 1

RICK: Very good. You're catching on.

CHARLOTTE: Oh..., I had no idea it had been sold. You must accept my deepest apologies. *(She fumbles in her pocket for the key, which she hands to Rick.)* I'm Charlotte, by the way, Charlotte Swift. *(She offers her hand.)*

VICKY: *(Shaking her hand)* Pleased to meet you, Mrs Swift.

CHARLOTTE: It's er... It's "Miss", actually, but you can call me "Charlotte".

RICK: *(Shaking hands)* Rick Maddocks. This is Vicky.

CHARLOTTE: Pleased to meet you... And here... Your key. I really had no idea someone was moving in.

(RICK takes the key.)

VICKY: Didn't you notice the light was on?

CHARLOTTE: Yes, of course I did..., but that's not unusual. The lights are often... *(She stops herself.)*

RICK: I suppose that's Mrs Whatever-Her-Name-Is. The young one. Does she use *your* key or has she got her own?

CHARLOTTE: *(Cagey)* You've... you've *seen* her?

RICK: Yes, she was here a few minutes ago.

CHARLOTTE: Is she still here?

VICKY: No. She ran off as soon as *I* came in.

CHARLOTTE: What about her husband? Was *he* here too?

RICK: No... Why?

CHARLOTTE: Ah... *(Deciding a quick exit is in order)* Well, I'd better be going. It was lovely to have met you both. I'm sorry to have intruded. I'll leave you in peace. *(She moves R.)*

VICKY: Wait! D'you know this woman?

CHARLOTTE: *(Turning)* No, no. I don't know her. I mean, I've never seen her.

VICKY: And what did *you* come here for?

CHARLOTTE: I er.... I... I was just keeping an eye on the place, that's all. But now *you're* here, well... I'll be off.

VICKY: Wait...!

(CHARLOTTE exits quickly R, slamming the front door as she goes. VICKY and RICK look at each other incredulously.)

VICKY: I wonder who *she* was?

RICK: *(Facing L)* God knows. At least she didn't try and throw us out.

VICKY: *(Facing him, holding hands)* Or seduce you.

(Unseen by Vicky and Rick, JESSICA enters slowly L.)

RICK: Ugh! Don't be disgusting!

VICKY: Oh, I see. It's all right for this other one to have a go at you, but not that

14

one!

RICK: Quite right. *(Changing the subject)* Well, we'd better get unpacked so we can get a night's sleep tonight.

(RICK notices Jessica. At the same moment VICKY's face changes to a worried expression. RICK breaks from Vicky and moves L.)

VICKY: *(Hugging herself)* Rick... I've gone cold again....

RICK: *(To Jessica)* So there you are! Where the hell did you get to?

(VICKY starts to look horrified as she observes Rick talking to nobody.)

RICK: This is my wife, Vicky. You never did say what your name was.

JESSICA: Jessica.

VICKY: Rick... What....!?

RICK: *(To Jessica)* Right! Now before you dash off again, I want to explain once and for all....

VICKY: Rick... Stop it! You're making me nervous. What are you doing?

RICK: I'm trying to explain to Jessica here that we bought this house....

VICKY: Rick... There's nobody there!

The Curtain falls.

ACT I Scene 2

Moments later. Everything is as it was at the end of Act I Scene 1

RICK: Vicky, what are you talking about?

VICKY: If this is supposed to be some sort of joke, Rick, it's not very funny.

RICK: Joke!? I don't understand.

JESSICA: She's getting cross, Ricky.

RICK: Don't call me "Ricky"!

JESSICA: Why not? It's a better name than Vicky... "Ricky and Vicky"... Yuk!

VICKY: I didn't.

RICK: Didn't what?

VICKY: Call you "Ricky". I hate the name.

JESSICA: Then I shall *always* use it!

RICK: I was talking to *her*.

VICKY: Stop it, Rick!

RICK: Stop what, for God's sake!?

VICKY: Just because I got nervous before, there's no need to play jokes on me.

RICK: Jokes...? Vicky, what the hell are you talking about?

VICKY: *(Increasingly angry)* I don't like it, Rick. You may think it's hilariously funny, but *I* don't.

RICK: *(Reacting)* What *are* you going on about?

VICKY: If you're going to be so cruel you can damn-well sleep on your own tonight! *I'm* going to unpack!

(VICKY storms off L. She nearly walks into JESSICA, who stands aside to let her pass. RICK follows Vicky, but she slams the door in his face.)

RICK: *(Confused)* Vicky...!

JESSICA: *(Amused)* You still don't understand, do you, Ricky?

RICK: *(Turning to face her)* Don't you talk to me. Can't you see what trouble you've caused?

JESSICA: *(Coming close in front of him)* I told you Vicky's a child's name. She even behaves like one.

RICK: *(Moving away)* Just leave her out of it.

JESSICA: *(Following)* How come you two ended up together? *(Musing)* "Vicky and Ricky"... "Ricky and Vicky"... Surely you could do better than *that*.

RICK: It's got nothing to do with you.

JESSICA: Oh, but it has.... You're in *my* house, remember?

RICK: Once and for all....

JESSICA: *(Undoing his tie)* And I have to look after my guests, don't I?

RICK: *(Trying to stop her)* Will you stop that!? My wife's upstairs!

Late Of This Address   ACT I Scene 2

JESSICA: *I* don't care.
RICK: *(Breaking away)* Well *I* do!
JESSICA: *(Sitting on the settee)* Come and sit with me.
RICK: No. I think you'd better go... Now!
JESSICA: Go where? This is my home.
RICK: Go wherever it is you went to last time.
JESSICA: I didn't go anywhere. I was here all the time.
RICK: *(Moving next to her)* Here...!? But I....
JESSICA: You're very slow, aren't you?
RICK: Am I?
JESSICA: Very. *(A pause.)* Vicky wasn't lying before, you know.
RICK: Lying? What about?
JESSICA: When she said there was nobody here.
RICK: *(Puzzled)* What're you talking about?
JESSICA: She can't see me.
RICK: Can't...?
JESSICA: And this house *has* been empty for the last twenty years.
RICK: *(Standing next to the settee)* But I thought you said...
JESSICA: *(Softly)* Ever since I died.
> *(RICK is speechless. He automatically sits down on the settee next to Jessica, then realises who or what she may be, leaps to his feet and takes a step back. JESSICA is highly amused.)*

JESSICA: I take it you don't believe in ghosts?
RICK: Ghosts...!? I... no... I...
JESSICA: I was born forty-three years ago. Don't you think I look young for my age?
RICK: This is ridiculous! You're no ghost! Ghosts do things like... *(He is about to describe his idea of what a ghost might be like, but stops himself.)*
JESSICA: What...? Walking through walls? Wandering around clanking chains and carrying their heads under their arms? I'm afraid not, Ricky. *(She stands and slowly twirls round.)* What you see is what you get.
RICK: But I can feel you, touch you.
JESSICA: *(Coming close to him and putting her arms round his neck)* And I can feel and touch you, too. *(She strokes his hair.)* Nice, eh?
RICK: But you're warm... Ghosts are supposed to be cold.
JESSICA: I think you'll find I'm far from cold.
> *(JESSICA tries to kiss Rick. He is about to respond as if hypnotised, but at the last moment realises what he is doing and breaks away.)*

RICK: Look, who the hell are you?

JESSICA: Oh, you are being tiresome, Ricky. Can't you believe what your eyes tell you?

RICK: I believe you're trying to pull some fast one. I don't know what you're after, but...

JESSICA: Company, that's what I'm after. Have you any idea what it's like being trapped in this house for twenty years and not seeing anyone? You should be flattered. You're the first one I've ever materialised to.

RICK: *(Insistent)* What d'you want!?

JESSICA: *(Stroking his cheek)* You, for starters...

RICK: *(Pushing her hand away)* Will you stop that!?

JESSICA: *(Decisive)* Alright, if you don't believe me I'll prove it to you... Call her down!

RICK: What?

JESSICA: Your wife... *(with disrespect)* What's-Her-Name.

RICK: Vicky.

JESSICA: Call her... I'll show you.

RICK: *(Dubious)* What're you going to do to her?

JESSICA: Nothing.

(RICK is still hesitant.)

JESSICA: I promise. She won't even know I'm here. Just call her down and tell her you're sorry. Don't say anything to me or about me. I give you my word... if she sees me I'll go away right now and never come back. If she doesn't.... well, you'll know I'm right, won't you?

RICK: *(Hesitant at first, but then determined)* Right! I will! *(He marches to the door L. Calling to off L)* Vicky!

VICKY: *(Off L; distant and frosty)* What?

RICK: Can you come down a minute?

VICKY: No!

RICK: Please.

VICKY: Not until you apologise.

RICK: All right. I'm sorry. Please come down.

(Footsteps can be heard descending the stairs. RICK moves L to stand L of Jessica. VICKY enters L and stands in front of him.)

VICKY: Well?

RICK: *(Embracing her)* I'm sorry, darling. I didn't mean to upset you.

VICKY: It wasn't very kind, was it? You knew I was frightened.

RICK: *(Facing her)* Forgive me?

Late Of This Address **ACT I Scene 2**

(JESSICA stands behind them and waves her hand directly in front of Vicky's eyes. VICKY does not notice a thing, looking into Rick's face just as before. RICK looks nervously at Jessica.)

JESSICA: See? She doesn't even know I'm here.

VICKY: Promise not to do it again?

RICK: *(Lovingly)* I promise.

(They embrace again, her head on his shoulder.)

JESSICA: *(Imitating; mocking)* I promise. Yuk! *(She reaches down and lifts the hem at the back of Vicky's skirt slightly, looks at it disdainfully, then drops it. Shaking her head)* Dreadful skirt!

VICKY: *(Shivering)* Brrh! *(She tugs her skirt down.)*

RICK: What?

VICKY: That draught again... It went right up my skirt.

(JESSICA plonks down on the settee, deliberately showing plenty of leg to distract Rick. He is quick to notice.)

RICK: *(Tearing his eyes from Jessica; tentatively)* Vicky...

VICKY: Mmmm?

RICK: D'you believe in ghosts?

JESSICA: *(Standing and moving L; warning)* Dangerous, Ricky! *Very* dangerous.

VICKY: *(Pulling apart)* Now don't start that again...! You promised...

RICK: No, I wasn't starting anything. I was just wondering, with you being so nervous and everything, whether that's what you were frightened of.

VICKY: I don't know *what* I was frightened of. I was just aware of an atmosphere. Cold and threatening.

RICK: *(Without thinking)* They're not *cold*.

VICKY: *(Nervous)* What!?

RICK: *(Quickly)* Er... Ghosts... Erm... that's what I've read. When people have claimed to have seen ghosts, that is.

VICKY: Well, that's what I felt. But, like you said, it was probably tiredness and draughts. *(She returns to his embrace.)*

RICK: Yes. *(A pause.)* D'you feel cold now?

(As VICKY replies, JESSICA moves close to her.)

VICKY: No. *(She suddenly shivers as Jessica moves next to her.)* Yes. *(She clutches at Rick. Panicky)* Rick! I can feel it again!

RICK: *(Ushering an amused Jessica away with his hand so without Vicky seeing)* Just a draught, Vicky. That's all. *(Lying)* I felt it too.

JESSICA: Liar!

VICKY: *(Still nervous)* Did you?

RICK: Yes... Better now?

VICKY: Mmmm.

JESSICA: Convinced? I'm warm if I like you, and very, *very* cold if I don't... *(Hostile)* And I *don't* like *her*...! She's a wimp!

(RICK is about to speak, but JESSICA holds her fingers to her lips quickly.)

Get rid of her!

(RICK glares at her.)

Go on. Send her upstairs or something. Then we can be alone.

(RICK mouths "No".)

I can quite easily frighten the pants off her if I want. A few cold breaths..., some moving furniture..., anything. *(Unseen by Vicky she picks up an ornament and threatens to throw it at her.)* I'm *very* good... I've had twenty years of practice.

(RICK raises a hand to stop her. JESSICA replaces the ornament and resumes her pose on the settee.)

RICK: Ah, well... Perhaps you'd better get on with the unpacking.

VICKY: *(Breaking L)* Yes, alright, darling. Aren't you coming up?

JESSICA: No, he's not, little girl. He's staying here with *me*!

RICK: I'll be up in a few minutes. I'll try and get the boiler going.

JESSICA: Easy. *(She snaps her finger and immediately there is a muffled pop as the boiler is heard to light off L.)* You only had to say.

VICKY: *(Looking off L)* What was that?

RICK: *(Moving to the door L and opening it)* It sounded like... *(He exits L.)*

VICKY: *(Moving to the door and calling)* Rick.... What is it...? Rick..!

RICK: *(Entering L, casting an uneasy glance at the smiling Jessica)* It was the boiler... It's come on.

VICKY: *(Worried)* But... but that's impossible...! *(Ominously)* Rick... I'm getting that feeling again.

(JESSICA laughs.)

RICK: *(Quickly)* It... it's alright. I er... I had a go at it when you were at the Off Licence. The timer must have clicked in.

(JESSICA applauds.)

JESSICA: Very good, Ricky! You *do* think fast.

RICK: I tried it before you got back, but... well it seems to be O.K. now. Go on... off you go.

JESSICA: Yes, off you go.., *(with disrespect)* Victoria. Ricky and I have some unfinished business!

__Late Of This Address__   __ACT I Scene 2__

(VICKY exits L.)

VICKY: *(As she goes)* Don't be long. Perhaps we can have a *proper* honeymoon night.

JESSICA: Aye, aye, Ricky..! Play your cards right and you could be in, there!

RICK: Right. Ten minutes at the most.

(VICKY exits L and can be heard going upstairs. RICK looks troubled and moves C.)

JESSICA: *(Standing and going to him)* Believe me now?

RICK: Either that or I'm going loopy!

JESSICA: You're sane as you ever were... Not that that's anything to go by.

RICK: What d'you mean?

JESSICA: However did you manage to get yourself saddled with a *drip* like that?

RICK: *(Offended)* Vicky!?

JESSICA: Yes... Vicky!

RICK: What've you got against her?

JESSICA: Everything. I don't like her.

RICK: Why? What has she ever done to you?

JESSICA: Moved into *my* house for one thing.

RICK: Even if it *is* your house, Vicky wasn't to know.

JESSICA: That's no excuse! And those clothes! So old-fashioned! Her skirt must be six inches past her knees!

RICK: *(Defending his wife)* It's *you* that's old-fashioned.

JESSICA: Me?

RICK: Yes, you.... Miniskirts went out years ago!

JESSICA: *(Disappointed)* Did they...? That's a shame. I'm glad *I'm* not alive today. *(After a pause where she draws her hem up to make sure her legs are being shown to their best advantage)* D'you think I've got nice legs?

RICK: *(Distracted by her display)* Oh, yes.

JESSICA: *(She pats the seat next to her)* Come and sit next to me.

(RICK is mesmerised and starts to do as she says. Just as he is about to sit he snaps back to reality and leaps up again.)

JESSICA: *(Exasperated) Now* what's the matter?

RICK: Vicky....

JESSICA: Not *her* again..!

RICK: She *is* my wife! I love her!

JESSICA: Well, *I* don't like her. *(She stands and moves to him.)* Now can't we just forget about her and....

Late Of This Address ACT I Scene 2

RICK: Does that mean you don't like *me* either?

JESSICA: *(Putting her arms round his neck again)* Oh, no... I like *you* a lot. I have totally different plans for *you*.

RICK: *(Struggling)* Stop that! Behave!

JESSICA: Why should I? Twenty years is a long time you know. It's nice to have a man around again. I'm a hot-blooded woman.

RICK: You *were*, you mean.

JESSICA: *(Unbuttoning his shirt collar)* I still am, as you could find out if you'd only stop trying to resist.
(Over the next few lines JESSICA becomes increasingly amorous with Rick, who does his best to avoid her and keep her talking with questions.)

RICK: What about your husband?

JESSICA: What about him?

RICK: What would he think of you carrying on like this?

JESSICA: *(With obvious disrespect for her husband)* Him!? How the hell should I know? I've not seen him for twenty years.

RICK: Is he still alive?

JESSICA: No. He died the same time as me.

RICK: Is he here too?
(RICK is backing towards the settee.)

JESSICA: If he is, I've never seen him. And even if I could he'd hardly be in a position to object.

RICK: Why?

JESSICA: Because throughout the three years we called our marriage he had a long succession of girlfriends.

RICK: He did?

JESSICA: Yes, he did.
(JESSICA pushes RICK, who falls back onto the settee.)

JESSICA: *(Climbing on his knee)* And now, at last, I've got a chance to get my own back!

RICK: *(Struggling but failing to get out from under her)* Get off! What the hell d'you think you're doing!?
(RICK manages to push her into a sitting position beside him.)

JESSICA: *(Sinister)* I could *make* you like me.

RICK: *(Uneasy)* What d'you mean?

JESSICA: It's easy. The same as I can make you feel hot...,
(RICK suddenly fells his collar, as if very hot.)

JESSICA: ...or cold.

Late Of This Address   ACT I Scene 2

(RICK shivers as if suddenly very cold. After a few moments JESSICA turns to face him and he is irresistibly drawn to her.)

JESSICA: It's a sort of hypnosis. *(Gently and persistently)* I can make you do anything I want. Anything at all.

(RICK is totally mesmerised, irresistibly staring into her eyes and moving his face slowly but surely towards hers. JESSICA suddenly breaks off and snaps them both back to reality with her next words.)

JESSICA: But it's no challenge!

RICK: *(Clearing his head)* What?

JESSICA: It's no fun at all. I want you to want me for myself. Of your own free will.

RICK: *(Starting to raise his voice)* When will you get it into your thick head? I'm married.

JESSICA: And when will you get it into *your* thick head? *(Slowly)* I don't care!

RICK: *(Angry)* You're immoral!

JESSICA: *(Responding in kind)* I'm entitled to be!

RICK: *(Remembering Vicky upstairs)* Shhh...! You'll bring Vicky down!

JESSICA: *(Still shouting)* I won't bring her down. She can't hear *me*, remember! But, yes... let's bring her down. Let's have a bit of fun. Call her.

RICK: *(Hushed)* No!

JESSICA: *(An order; slowly and firmly)* Do as I say!

(RICK is unable to resist. He goes to the door L and calls.)

RICK: *(In a flat tone)* Vicky...! Come down a minute.

VICKY: *(Off L)* What... now?

JESSICA: Say nothing! *(In the same persuasive tone)* Come and sit here. *(She pats the settee.)*

(RICK sits where he is directed. JESSICA stands and then sits on his knee. She puts her arms round his neck. The door L opens and VICKY appears. She wears a dressing gown.)

VICKY: Were you calling me?

RICK: *(Confused)* Yes, I.... *(He breaks off.)*

VICKY: *(Moving C)* Well?

JESSICA: Tell her I'm here.

RICK: *(Blindly)* She's here, Vicky.

VICKY: *(Wondering what he can be talking about)* What...? Who's here?

RICK: Jessica.

VICKY: Who's Jessica?

RICK: The one I told you about... The one who claims she owns...

23

Late Of This Address   **ACT II Scene 1**

JESSICA: *(Interrupting)* I *do* own it!
RICK: The one who owns the house.
VICKY: *(Getting annoyed again)* Rick!
RICK: *(Insistent)* She's here!
VICKY: Have you been at that brandy I bought?
RICK: No I haven't!
VICKY: If you're trying to scare me again, you're succeeding.
RICK: I mean it, Vicky.
VICKY: *(Taking a deep breath)* This isn't funny, Rick.
RICK: I'm not trying to be funny, Vicky. She's here... sitting on my knee.
VICKY: What!?
RICK: She's a ghost!
JESSICA: I prefer "spirit" myself, but let it pass.
VICKY: *(Hostile)* Rick..! Why are you doing this?
JESSICA: Tell her you'll prove it to her.
RICK: I'll prove it to you.
VICKY: *(Frosty)* This should be *very* interesting!
   (JESSICA starts to undo Rick's shirt. Gradually a look of horror appears on VICKY's face. She backs away.)
VICKY: Rick..! What...!?
RICK: It's all right, Vicky. She won't hurt you.
JESSICA: Yet!
VICKY: Where... Where is she?
JESSICA: *(Still unbuttoning his shirt)* I should have thought that was obvious. I'm over here, *(with venom)* Vicky, making love to your husband!
RICK: I told you... she's sitting on my knee.
VICKY: *(Panicky)* Get away from her...! Rick...! Please!
RICK: I'd like to, Vicky, honestly I would, but...
   (His words are muffled as JESSICA kisses him fully on the mouth. VICKY screams and dashes off R. RICK and JESSICA slowly lie back on the settee as the CURTAIN falls.)

ACT II Scene 1

It is the following morning. As the curtain rises, RICK is asleep on the settee. He is under a blanket, and is stripped to the waist. A car is heard to draw up off R. After a moment a key is heard in the front door off R, which then opens and slams. RICK starts to wake up. VICKY, in a foul mood, enters R. She carries their car keys.

RICK: *(As he spots Vicky)* Oh, hello.

VICKY: *(Hostile)* Hello!? Is that all you can say... "Hello"!?

RICK: *(Not knowing why she is upset)* Why....? What...?

VICKY: I've come for my things.

RICK: What things?

VICKY: My clothes. I'm going back to Vera's.

RICK: *(Rising; shocked)* You're *what*!?

VICKY: You heard!

RICK: This is a joke, right?

VICKY: If it is, it's about as funny as last night!

RICK: Vicky, will you tell me what the hell you're talking about?

VICKY: Oh, don't come that innocent air with me, Rick! *(She storms L.)*

RICK: Innocent...? *(As she moves towards the door L)* Vicky...! Vicky!

VICKY: *(Stopping at the door L and steeling herself; through gritted teeth)* What!?

RICK: *(Genuinely confused)* Tell me... Whatever I've done I'll apologise, but I honestly can't remember what it is.

(VICKY turns to face him, about to let him have a tirade of abuse, but she realises he is genuine.)

VICKY: You *really* can't remember?

RICK: No.

VICKY: What *do* you remember? About last night?

RICK: I remember you going out to the off licence for something..., then you came back and.... I must have dozed off.

VICKY: So you don't remember her?

RICK: Her?

VICKY: Our visitor.

RICK: Visitor...? *(Suddenly remembering)* Oh.... Yes, I *do* remember. Now what was her name...? Charlotte! That's it!

VICKY: Not her!

RICK: *(Puzzled)* Not her?

VICKY: What about our *other* visitor?

Late Of This Address   **ACT II Scene 1**

RICK: Other visitor?

VICKY: Rick, if I'd wanted a parrot I'd have bought one!

RICK: *(Even more confused)* Parrot?

VICKY: *(Impatient)* Oh, for God's sake...! What about the *other* visitor?

RICK: I don't remember any other visitor. Vicky, are you trying to tell me I lost my memory, or blacked out, or something?

VICKY: I only wish I was.

RICK: Remind me.

VICKY: Jessica!

RICK: *(Instantly remembering; eyes wide)* Jessica..! Yes!

VICKY: So you *do* remember.

RICK: Some of it, yes. My God... I thought it was a dream.

VICKY: Is she here?

RICK: *(Looking anxiously around)* No.

VICKY: Check the rest of the house.

RICK: *(Rising; nervous)* Do I have to?

VICKY: Yes, you do.

RICK: Will you come with me?

VICKY: No... *I* can't see her, remember?

(RICK goes nervously to the door L, opens it slightly and peers through. He looks nervously back at Vicky.)

VICKY: *(Whispering)* Go on!

(RICK exits L, leaving the door open. VICKY keeps glancing anxiously round the room. She shivers suddenly with cold, which frightens her. RICK enters L, leaving the door open.)

VICKY: Well...?

RICK: No sign of her.

VICKY: Is she.... Are you *sure* she's not in here?

RICK: *(Looking round)* No... I told you. Why?

VICKY: I suddenly went cold.

RICK: Probably a draught.

VICKY: Now don't start that again. Whenever I went cold last night she was here.

RICK: Well, if she is, *I* can't see her. *(He sits on the L seat of the settee.)*

VICKY: What're we going to do, Rick?

RICK: Where did you sleep last night?

VICKY: At the Swan in the village.

RICK: I still can't remember what happened. How did I come to be sleeping here?

VICKY: *(She sits next to him. Dubious)* You're *sure* you're not making all this up?

RICK: Positive. Tell me what happened.

VICKY: She... this *Jessica*... seemed to have some sort of hold on you. You behaved like a complete pig.

RICK: Did you see her?

VICKY: No. But I saw what was happening to you.

RICK: What did I do?

VICKY: It's not so much what *you* did. More what *she* did. *(She pauses.)*

RICK: *(Impatient to know)* Well... Are you going to tell me or not?

VICKY: She... You said she was sitting on your knee. Next thing I knew your clothes were coming off all on their own!

RICK: *(Looking at his bare chest)* You mean she...! *(Aghast)* Then what happened?

VICKY: I don't know. I was scared stiff. I just ran. I got in the car and headed off as fast as I could.

RICK: Yes... I vaguely remember that... Thanks for deserting me.

VICKY: You didn't seem as if you wanted to leave. Marvellous, isn't it!? Married six weeks and my husband goes off with someone I can't even see!

RICK: I *didn't* go off with her! She... she seems to have some sort of.. hypnotic control. It's very difficult to resist her.

VICKY: So you *can* remember what happened!?

RICK: Bits keep coming back to me. Like I dreamt them.

VICKY: *(Steeling herself)* Did she...? That is, did you and she...? You know.

RICK: *(Indignant)* No we didn't! *(After a pause)* At least I don't *think* we did.

VICKY: What does she want?

RICK: Me, from what she was saying.

VICKY: You?

RICK: Her husband was apparently a bit of a womaniser. She wants revenge.

VICKY: And she's chosen you as the instrument?

RICK: So it seems.

VICKY: And where do *I* fit into this little mess?

RICK: You don't. She doesn't like you.

VICKY: The feeling is mutual.

RICK: I wish I knew what to do.

VICKY: We've got to get out, Rick.

Late Of This Address   **ACT II Scene 1**

RICK: We can't. This is our house... our dream.

VICKY: Looks like *your* dream is turning into *my* nightmare!

RICK: *(Sourly)* Very poetic!

VICKY: We must leave. Right now. Perhaps we can go into the village and see the vicar. They're supposed to know about these things, aren't they? Perhaps he could do an exorcism or something and get her out.

RICK: *(Defiant)* I *refuse* to be driven out of *my* house by a dead person!

VICKY: We've got no choice. I don't know what control she had over you last night, but it terrifies me. She could get you to do *anything*. I'd never be safe.

RICK: *(Hurt)* Vicky! You know I'd never do anything to hurt you.

VICKY: But *she* would. We've got to go, to get help. Put your shirt on.

RICK: *(Standing and putting his shirt on)* How about if we go back to the estate agent and see if anyone else has ever seen anything here?

VICKY: They'll think you're mad.

RICK: We could go to the library and find out a bit more about the place. That might help the vicar.

VICKY: Alright, but come on... let's get out.

(VICKY takes RICK's hand and they move quickly towards the door R. As Vicky reaches the door, JESSICA enters through the open door L.)

JESSICA: *(Holding up her hand to stop Rick)* Stop!

(RICK stops dead. He is still holding Vicky's hand and his sudden halt stops her before she can exit.)

VICKY: Come on! *(She notices Rick has stopped still.)* Rick..!? What...?

JESSICA: You didn't really think I'd let you go, did you?

RICK: *(Looking at Vicky; unable to move)* Vicky...! It's her! She's here.

VICKY: *(Trying to pull him R)* Come on, then!

RICK: I can't! I can't move!

JESSICA: Of course you can, Ricky...! But not that way.

(RICK finds he is able to move L, but cannot move any nearer the door R.)

VICKY: Rick! What's happening!?

RICK: *(Hopelessly)* I can't get out, Vicky. She won't let me. You go... get out while you can!

VICKY: *(Ready to fight)* I'm not letting her have you.

RICK: Don't upset her. You don't know what she can do!

VICKY: *(Looking wildly round the room)* Where are you, you bitch!?

JESSICA: *(Chiding)* Now, now, Victoria! That's not very ladylike, is it?

RICK: Leave her alone, damn you!

JESSICA: Too late! I'm already damned!

Late Of This Address	ACT II Scene 1

VICKY: Where is she, Rick?
RICK: Don't hurt her!
JESSICA: Don't worry, she's not worth the effort.
VICKY: Rick! Speak to me! Where is she?
RICK: By the door.
VICKY: *(Moving towards the door L and talking towards where she thinks Jessica might be)* Look, I don't know who you are, and I don't honestly give a damn.
RICK: Vicky, don't...
(Before RICK can say any more, JESSICA snaps her fingers and no matter how hard he tries he is unable to speak.)
JESSICA: *(Moving to him)* Let her talk, Ricky. It amuses me.
VICKY: *(Still talking to the door)* If you think I'm going to give up my husband and our house to some trollop...
JESSICA: *(Amused)* Trollop!?
VICKY: ...then you've got another think coming. I'll fight you all the way. I swear I will.
JESSICA: Fight...!? With what? I could swat you like a fly.
VICKY: So leave us alone. If you know what's good for you.
JESSICA: *(To Rick)* Now she's beginning to bore me. *(She moves to the door L. To Rick)* See you later darling.... *(With a smile)* Don't go away, will you?
VICKY: I don't know how I can fight you, but I will. There must be a way, and sooner or later I'll find it.
(RICK is suddenly released from silence. He holds his throat, finding it a strain to speak at first.)
RICK: *(A croak)* She's gone!
VICKY: *(Turning to face him)* Where?
RICK: Out there. Wherever she goes.
VICKY: Go and check.
(RICK checks the door L. He comes back and shakes his head. He feels his throat as if it is sore.)
VICKY: *(Moving to the door R)* Come on then! Before she comes back.
(RICK attempts to go to the door R, but can reach no further than before, as if trying to break through an invisible wall. He feels the "wall" with his hands.)
RICK: I can't, Vicky. I just can't.
VICKY: Fight it, Rick! There's nothing there! You must believe that!
RICK: I *do* believe it! I can *see* there's nothing there. But I *still* can't move!
VICKY: *(Moving quickly to the door L)* Let's try the back way. Come on.
(RICK follows her quickly off L. They return, dejected, a few moments later.)

Late Of This Address   **ACT II Scene 1**

RICK: It's no use, Vicky. I'm stuck here.

VICKY: What about the windows?

RICK: You know it won't work as well as I do. You'll have to get help on your own.

VICKY: No... That's just what she wants. I am *not* leaving here without you.

RICK: Then I suppose we'll just have to wait to see what she does next... If only we were on the phone. We could ring someone for help.

VICKY: Like who?

RICK: *(Desperate; shaking his head)* I don't know.... I really don't.

VICKY: There must be *something* we can do.

RICK: Any suggestions?

VICKY: Look around. Let's see if there's any papers, or diaries, or... anything. *(She starts looking in the sideboard drawers.)*

RICK: What for?

VICKY: *I* don't know! Maybe they could give us a clue as to who she is. It helps if we know who we're dealing with. If we could find out a bit more about her perhaps we could find a way to persuade her to let us go.

RICK: *(Glum)* Some hope!

VICKY: *(Cross)* Well it's better than just sitting around moping. Come on... you look over there.

(RICK goes wearily to the mantlepiece and looks in and under the ornaments. VICKY checks all the drawers and cupboards in the sideboard.)

VICKY: Anything?

RICK: Nothing.... You?

(VICKY shakes her head. As she closes the bottom sideboard drawer she notices Charlotte's book on the floor.)

VICKY: Wait a minute... What's this? *(She picks up the book and reads the title.)* "The Spirit World - The Paranormal Explained" by Walter Stein. I wonder...

(VICKY opens the book and starts to read. She moves to the settee and sits. RICK sits next to her.)

RICK: What is it?

VICKY: What it says... A book about the paranormal. Listen to this... *(She reads)* "Walter Stein is an outspoken authority on the world of spirits and the supernatural. His books have challenged the beliefs of traditional psychics and mediums, but the results of his methods are without equal."

(VICKY continues looking through the book over the next few lines.)

RICK: I've never heard of him.

VICKY: So what? Why should *we* have heard of him?

Late Of This Address   **ACT II Scene 1**

RICK: It's a bit suspicious finding it here.

VICKY: Why is it? The place is haunted. There's probably been hundreds of cranks crawling all over it. Anyone could have left it here.

RICK: Perhaps *she* left it here... Jessica.

VICKY: Why?

RICK: How should *I* know? Maybe it's a trap.

VICKY: We're already trapped. *(She reads; after a moment)* "Chapter Nine - The Exorcism" *(She turns to Chapter Nine.)* "There is no evidence that the traditional exorcism as practised by the clergy over the past few centuries is effective. On many occasions the result has been to enrage the presence..."

RICK: "Presence"?

VICKY: He probably means the ghost. "Where the exorcism has been effective, the results are seldom permanent, so that - sometimes within a period of hours - the presence returns, frequently stronger."

RICK: I think he's telling us not to dabble. Perhaps we should...

VICKY: Shhh! I'm only reading.... I didn't say I was going to *do* anything... "An effective and permanent method involves the waving of a cross in a room frequented by the presence. At the same time the person waving the cross must recant three times - and three times only - 'In the name of this cross and the power within, spirit return to whence you came'."

RICK: What a load of rot!

VICKY: How d'you know?

RICK: You don't actually *believe* all that, do you?

VICKY: If you'd asked me two days ago I'd have said "No". Today I'm not so sure.

RICK: Put it down, Vicky. You don't know what you're playing with.

VICKY: *(Standing and looking round the room)* We need a cross.

RICK: Vicky! I thought you said you weren't going to do anything.

VICKY: *(Looking at the book)* It says here that a cross can be "fashioned from any suitable material at hand. Even crossed sticks will do."

RICK: Sounds like one of those old vampire movies.

VICKY: I know. *(She returns to the sideboard and takes two table knives from a drawer.)* These'll do.

RICK: Vicky...! You can't!

VICKY: What choice do we have? Now...

(VICKY stands down R and holds the two knives in her right hand so as to make a cross. She holds the book in her left hand and reads the chant.)

VICKY: "In the name of this cross and the power within, spirit return to whence you came."... "In the name of this cross and the power within, spirit return to

Late Of This Address　　　　　　　　ACT II Scene 2

whence you came."
(During the third reading of the chant JESSICA enters L. She looks in horror at what Vicky is doing.)
JESSICA: *(Moving towards Vicky, her voice a wail)* No! Stop it! *(To Rick; furious)* Make her stop it!
RICK: What...?
(Before RICK can react to JESSICA's demand VICKY repeats the line.)
VICKY: "In the name of this cross and the power within, spirit return to whence you came."
JESSICA: *(Enraged)* No...! No...! *(She stamps the room in rage.)*
RICK: *(Watching Jessica; to Vicky)* Something's happening.
VICKY: *(Moving to him)* What...? Tell me! Has she gone?
RICK: Not exactly.
VICKY: Then what?
RICK: She's not very pleased.
VICKY: I wonder how long it takes to work?
JESSICA: *(Still wailing)* What have you done?
RICK: *(To Jessica)* You can't say you didn't deserve it.
JESSICA: None of us deserve this.
VICKY: *(Starting to be amused)* Is she getting upset?
RICK: You could say that.
VICKY: Serves her right!
JESSICA: *(Facing up to Vicky)* Why...!? You *stupid* bitch! Why couldn't you just leave it alone!?
(RONNIE ambles through the door L. He is yawning and stretching as if he has awakened from a long sleep.)
RONNIE: *(Seeing Jessica)* Who are these people, Jessie?
JESSICA: *(With weary acceptance)* Hello, Ronnie!
VICKY: Who on earth are you?
RICK: *(Looking round; mystified)* Vicky...! Who the hell are you talking to?
(Quick CURTAIN)

ACT II Scene 2

A moment later. (It is essential that the next few lines be played at a fast pace.)

JESSICA: *(To Rick; weary)* Ricky, this is my husband, Ronnie.

RONNIE: *(Not really interested in Rick; impatient to get an explanation from Jessica)* Hi. Pleased to meet you.... Look, Jessie...

RICK: *(To Jessica)* What are you talking about?

VICKY: *(To Rick)* What are *you* talking about? And *who's* this?

RICK: *(To Vicky)* Who?

JESSICA: *(To Rick)* She means *him*!

RICK: *(Insistent)* Who?

VICKY: *(To Rick)* Him!

RONNIE: *(To Jessica)* Who are *they*?

JESSICA: Oh, don't *you* start!

RICK: *(To Jessica)* Don't *who* start!?

VICKY: *(To Rick)* What?

JESSICA: *(To herself)* Oh, this is ridiculous!

RONNIE: *(To Jessica)* What is?

VICKY: *(To Ronnie)* What is what?

RICK: What?

JESSICA: *(Moving to Rick)* Don't you see what you've done!?

RONNIE: Who?

VICKY: *(To Ronnie)* Who what?

JESSICA: *(To Ronnie)* You stay out of this. I'll explain everything.

RICK: I wish someone would!

VICKY: *(To Rick)* You wish someone would what? Rick, what's going on...?

RICK: *(To Vicky)* You stay out of this. She's going to explain everything.

VICKY: You mean she's still here!?

JESSICA: *(Impatient)* Tell her to shut up, for God's sake!

RICK: *(He is just about to do so, but thinks better of it.)* Yes... Shhh!

VICKY: But who...?

RICK: *(Firmer)* Shhh!

JESSICA: *(To Rick)* Where did you get that book?

RICK: We found it over there. Why... is it yours?

JESSICA: No, it isn't! *(She shakes her head in disbelief.)* Why did you have to go and meddle in things you don't understand?

RICK: Why....? What...?

JESSICA: That incantation.

Late Of This Address ACT II Scene 2

RICK: We were just trying to get rid of you. You mustn't take it personally, we just wanted our house back.

JESSICA: But you haven't got it, have you?

RICK: Well, no..., but, as they say, nothing ventured...

JESSICA: You tried to get rid of your troubles, and all you succeeded in doing is doubling them.

RICK: *Doubling* them!? I don't understand.

VICKY: Rick... What...?

RICK: *(To Vicky)* Shhh!

RONNIE: Jessie...!

JESSICA: *(To Ronnie)* Shhh!

VICKY: Rick, will you please tell me...

JESSICA: *(Together)* Shhh!
RICK:

JESSICA: All your little incantation achieved is to materialise my *(sarcastic)* poor, dear, departed husband!

RICK: *(Looking around; confused)* What...?

JESSICA: Except that *you* can't see him.

RICK: You mean he's here.... now...?

(JESSICA nods.)

RICK: Can *you* see him?

JESSICA: *(Looking at Ronnie disapprovingly)* Yes... Unfortunately. And what's even worse is that it appears your dear wife can also see him!

RICK: Vicky?

VICKY: What? What're you saying about me? What's *she* saying?

(RICK is about to say "Shhh" again.)

VICKY: And don't you dare "shush" me!

RICK: *(Going to Vicky)* You're not going to believe this.

VICKY: Try me.

RICK: Your little incantation... It failed.

VICKY: So I gather.... But I intend to try again, believe me!

RICK: No, don't do that for heaven's sake! You'll only make things worse.

JESSICA: If that's possible!

VICKY: How can they get worse!?

RICK: They already have. You've materialised her husband!

VICKY: I've what!?

RICK: You've materialised...

34

Late Of This Address   ACT II Scene 2

VICKY: *(Interrupting)* I *heard* what you said! *(Looking at Ronnie)* You mean this... this is...

RONNIE: *(Stepping towards her)* Pleased to meet you. I'm Ronnie. *(He extends his hand.)*

VICKY: *(Shaking his hand; stunned)* Likewise, I'm sure.

RICK: What?

VICKY: *(To Rick)* He's very polite.

JESSICA: *(To Vicky)* You don't know him like I do.

RICK: *(Turning to Jessica)* What?

VICKY: *(To Rick)* What?

JESSICA: *(To Rick)* Go on. Tell her the rest.

RICK: It seems that *your* incantation...

VICKY: Less of the *"your"*..! It was your idea too!

(VICKY puts the book on the sideboard.)

RICK: *(Aghast)* Mine!?

VICKY: *(Ready for a fight)* Ours, then!

RICK: *(Impatient)* Alright, alright! *Our* incantation has made it so *you* can see and hear *him*... and, as you know, *I* can see and hear *her*, but I *can't* see or hear him, and *you* can't see or hear *her*.

VICKY: Can they see each other?

JESSICA: *(To Vicky)* Of course we can, you pathetic little moron! How else would I know he's here?

RONNIE: *(To Jessica)* Your language hasn't improved, has it?

JESSICA: Bugger off, Ronnie!

RICK: Yes. Apparently they can.

VICKY: *(Going Ronnie)* So you're a ghost?

RONNIE: So it would seem.

RICK: *(To Vicky)* I thought you were scared of ghosts.

VICKY: So did I.... Before.

RICK: Before what?

VICKY: Before I met one... In the flesh.

JESSICA: *(To Ronnie)* I want to talk to you!

RONNIE: And I to you, Jessie, dear.

JESSICA: And *don't* call me "Jessie"! I hated it when I was alive, and...

RONNIE: *(Finishing for her)* ...you *haven't* improved!

JESSICA: And I *still* hate it!

RONNIE: Sorry... Jessie!

Late Of This Address ACT II Scene 2

RICK: *(To Vicky)* Are you getting all this?
VICKY: Not really.... You?
RICK: No. Half of it, but it doesn't make sense.
VICKY: *(Amused)* Nor does the other half! What *have* we done?
JESSICA: *(Advancing on Vicky; acidic)* I'm glad you find it amusing, *Vicky*! You may not be able to see me, but I could make life very unpleasant for you if I wanted.
RONNIE: *(Together)* You leave her alone!
RICK:
VICKY: Wow! It seems I have two champions! Is she threatening me?
RONNIE: Yes!
RICK: No!
RONNIE: *(After a curious look at Rick)* Yes! Now look here, Jessie..!
JESSICA: We need to talk.
RONNIE: *(To Vicky; the perfect gentleman)* Excuse us. We need to talk. *(He turns to Jessica.)*
VICKY: Don't let us keep you. We'll wander off down to the pub.
RICK: I can't..., remember?
VICKY: *(Wildly, to where she thinks Jessica might be)* Yoo-hoo! Jessica, wherever you are. Will you let me have my husband for an hour or two?
JESSICA: *(Angry)* No, I won't!
RICK: No, she won't.
RONNIE: Let them go, Jessie.
VICKY: We'll come back. Honestly. This *is* our house, after all.
JESSICA: *(To Ronnie)* No! I'm not letting him go! Not till we decide what to do.
RICK: Looks like we're stuck here, Vicky.
VICKY: *You* may be... *I'm* not! *(She turns and walks R.)*
JESSICA: *(To Ronnie)* Stop her!
RONNIE: How!?
JESSICA: Just *think* it!
(RONNIE turns to face Vicky and concentrates. VICKY stops abruptly and cannot go any further.)
RICK: *(Sarcastic)* What's the matter, Vicky? I thought you were leaving!
VICKY: *(Spitting)* Damn you, you bitch! Wherever you are!
JESSICA: *(To Rick)* See what you married, Ricky? Hardly the demure little wife, is she?
RICK: *(Thoughtful)* No.

Late Of This Address   **ACT II Scene 2**

JESSICA: *(Rounding on Ronnie)* Now, to deal with you!

RONNIE: What I want to know is what the hell is going on?

JESSICA: You've been materialised, my darling!

RONNIE: Is that good?

JESSICA: Bad... *Very* bad.

RONNIE: *(Yawning)* I'm shattered... What time is it?

VICKY: *(Glancing at her watch)* Ten fifteen.

RONNIE: *(To Vicky)* Thanks. *(After a thought)* What *year* is it?

JESSICA: *(Impatient)* Nineteen eighty-six! Now listen...!

RONNIE: *(Aghast)* Nineteen eighty-six!?

JESSICA: Yes. You've been dead for twenty years.

RONNIE: I have?

JESSICA: And, up until now, you've been dead and *gone*. Now, thanks to these two do-it-yourself psychics, you're dead and back again!

RONNIE: *(Dry)* You've not changed much in twenty years.

JESSICA: No. Nor have you. You're still as disgusting as you ever were.

RICK: *(To Vicky)* Looks like they're having a domestic!

VICKY: Yes... I feel like I'm prying. I'd leave..., if I could.

JESSICA: *(Rounding on them)* Can't you two shut up!?

RICK: Why should we? It's our house.

RONNIE: *Their* house!? Did you sell up?

JESSICA: No, I didn't! As far as the living are concerned, this house is empty and has been since we died. I've always managed to scare off anybody who's ever shown any interest... until now. Normally a few bangs, crashes and flashing lights - plus a cold breeze or two - has been enough. That *did* attract a few ghost-hunters over the years, but if you keep quiet they usually get bored and go away.

RONNIE: But it obviously didn't work with these two, did it?

VICKY: *(To Ronnie)* What didn't?

RICK: *(To Vicky)* What didn't what?

JESSICA: Oh, for God's sake don't lets start all that again! *(To Ronnie)* No, as you point out, it didn't work. *(Full of regret)* All because I was lonely and fed up and wanted a man in my life again.

RONNIE: *(Mocking)* Jessie, darling... You should have called me.

JESSICA: *(Venomous)* I said "a man", not a pig!

RONNIE: *(To Rick)* Why did you have to do it...? There I was, peacefully minding my own business...

JESSICA: *(Interrupting)* He can't hear you.

RONNIE: *(Moving to Vicky)* Why did you have to do it...? There I was, peacefully minding my own business, and all of a sudden I'm here, under the thumb again. *(He glances ruefully at Jessica.)*

JESSICA: *(To Ronnie)* You needn't look at me like that! *I* never wanted you back. *I* tried to stop them! I just wanted.... *(She suddenly stops and cranes her head towards off R.)* Someone's coming! *(She concentrates again.)* Up the path. *(Suddenly very angry)* Oh, God! What in *hell* can she want?

RONNIE: *(Pointing "down to hell")* So *that's* where you went, was it? I'm not surprised.

(There is a knock on the door off R.)

VICKY: *(Moving R)* Shall *I* go? *(She is stopped by the invisible barrier. She turns back into the room.)* Then again, perhaps not.

JESSICA: It's that blasted woman again!

RONNIE: What woman?

RICK: What woman?

JESSICA: That old bag from the village.

RONNIE: Who?

JESSICA: She reckons she's a psychic.

RONNIE: And is she?

JESSICA: A bloody nosey parker's more like. *(To Rick)* You'll have to get rid of her.

RICK: Why me?

VICKY: What?

RICK: Why do *I* have to get rid of her? If you're so damned good, why don't *you* scare her off?

JESSICA: Don't you think I've tried!? The old bat's too stupid to be scared.

RONNIE: Can *I* try?

JESSICA: No. *You'd* never do it.

RONNIE: You never did have much faith in my abilities, did you?

JESSICA: No... *(With meaning)* I used to sleep with you remember?

RONNIE: I never had any other complaints!

JESSICA: You two'll have to get rid of her. Ronnie, come with me!

RONNIE: Why..? Can't I stay and watch?

JESSICA: *(Firmly)* No!

(There is another - louder - knock at the front door off R.)

RONNIE: Why not?

JESSICA: Because *I* can't scare her off and *I've* had twenty years experience. The last three of them with *her*!

RONNIE: *(Realising)* You're scared, aren't you?

JESSICA: No, course not!

RONNIE: Yes you are! I've seen you like this before!

JESSICA: It's just that she...

RONNIE: What?

JESSICA: There's something strange about her. I think she may be able to see me.

RICK: Wonderful! Let's call her in!

VICKY: Rick... What's she saying? What's going on?

JESSICA: *(Furious)* No! Just get rid of her!

RICK: *(Sensing a victory)* Or what?

JESSICA: *(Threatening)* Or I'll *never* let you out of this house. Either of you.

RICK: *(Defiant)* We'll find a way sooner or later.

JESSICA: *(Glaring at him; threatening)* Don't underestimate the power of things you can't even begin to understand, Ricky!

RICK: I'm beginning to understand....

(RICK's words are suddenly cut off as JESSICA raises her hand towards him. In time with the closing of her fingers, RICK starts to feel tight around the throat and finds it difficult to breathe.)

VICKY: *(Seeing his predicament; wildly towards "Jessica")* Leave him alone, damn you! *(Appealing to Ronnie)* Do something! Make her stop! We'll do what you want... anything.

(JESSICA lowers her hand and RICK is released. He rubs his neck.)

JESSICA: Good boy. Now get rid of her.

RICK: *(Hoarse)* How? I can't just tell her to go. She'll be more suspicious than ever.

JESSICA: Do whatever it takes. And try and find out how much she knows, or *thinks* she knows.

RICK: *(Taking a step R)* You'll have to let me get to the door.

JESSICA: You'll find you can get to the door.... But no further! *(To Ronnie)* You... come with me! *(She exits L.)*

(RICK exits gingerly R, expecting to hit the invisible barrier. RONNIE moves towards the door L, but suddenly get an idea. He looks from his hand to Vicky and back again, then raises his hand towards her. VICKY tenses. He beckons with his hand and she is irresistibly drawn to him. He "draws" her face to his and kisses her.)

JESSICA: *(Off L)* Ronnie! Come on!

(RONNIE breaks the kiss and looks delighted with himself. He looks at his hand and smiles at his new-found power.)

Late Of This Address ACT II Scene 2

RONNIE: *(To Vicky)* I'll see *you* later.

(RONNIE exits L and closes the door. VICKY breaks from her trance. She puts her hand to her lips, clearly remembering what happened and not at all upset about it. RICK enters R with CHARLOTTE.)

RICK: *(Noticing Vicky's distracted expression)* Vicky... Are you O.K?

VICKY: *(Coming round)* What...? Oh..., yes, I'm fine. *(With a smile)* Fine.

RICK: Miss Swift has just called....

CHARLOTTE: *(Correcting him)* Charlotte, please, young man. *(She is facing Vicky.)*

RICK: Sorry..., *Charlotte* has lost one of her books. She thinks she may have dropped it here.

(RICK shakes his head to Vicky to indicate she should say nothing. VICKY looks puzzled, but says nothing.)

CHARLOTTE: *(Turning to Rick)* Stupid of me I know, but it was such a shock seeing you here. I'm most dreadfully sorry to keep pestering you like this.

(While Charlotte's back is turned VICKY manages to retrieve the book from the top of the sideboard and hide it underneath again.)

RICK: Not at all. We're always glad to see our neighbours, aren't we, Vicky?

VICKY: What...!? Oh, yes. Yes, of course. *(To Charlotte)* I'm forgetting my manners. Would you like to sit down?

CHARLOTTE: *(Fussing)* Oh, no, no... I couldn't put you to any trouble.

RICK: It's no trouble. Please.

(CHARLOTTE sits on the chair. VICKY sits of the settee.)

VICKY: Sorry if the chair's a bit damp.

CHARLOTTE: No, no... I like it. It give the place.... atmosphere.

RICK: Have you lived in the village long?

CHARLOTTE: About three years. I lived at Cottingbury most of my life, but now I room with Mrs Padstow in the village. Perhaps you know her.

RICK: No. We're strangers to the area.

VICKY: D'you know this house well?

CHARLOTTE: Well?

VICKY: Yes... You said you'd been looking after the place.

CHARLOTTE: Did I?

VICKY: Yes. That's why you had a key.

CHARLOTTE: Ah, yes... I er... I have.

RICK: You don't seem very sure.

CHARLOTTE: You're not annoyed?

VICKY: Why should we be annoyed? It wasn't our house until a few days ago.

Late Of This Address   **ACT II Scene 2**

RICK: *(Sotto voce)* And we're still not sure.
CHARLOTTE: I beg your pardon?
VICKY: *(Quickly)* We're still not sure whether we were wise to buy it.
RICK: But it's all we could afford.
CHARLOTTE: I see.
VICKY: Perhaps you could tell us a bit about the place.
CHARLOTTE: *(Cagey)* Like what?
RICK: Well, for example, d'you know anything about the previous occupants?
CHARLOTTE: Why do you ask that?
VICKY: We heard that a couple lived here years ago, but Mrs Eastwood - that's the Estate Agent - said it had been empty for twenty years. We're just curious.
CHARLOTTE: *(Reaching a decision)* Can we put our cards on the table, as it were?
VICKY: What d'you mean?
CHARLOTTE: You know, don't you? You've seen things.
RICK: Seen things?
CHARLOTTE: I've seen them, too. The lights going on and off... things not being where you left them... bangs and crashes... They think I'm mad in the village, but you have, haven't you? You've seen things too?
VICKY: Yes, we have.
CHARLOTTE: *(Delighted)* Oh, this is wonderful! Wonderful! Tell me all about it!
RICK: Well, first of all...
VICKY: *(She glares at him. Quickly; interrupting him)* It was just like you said... Lights, bangs, things moving.
CHARLOTTE: You've not seen *them*, have you?
RICK: *Them*?
CHARLOTTE: The people who lived here.
VICKY: *(Firmly)* No... No, we haven't!
CHARLOTTE: Ah... Pity.
RICK: Who were they?
CHARLOTTE: From what I've been able to find out - from the papers of the time and by talking to people in the village - a young couple lived here. Newlyweds, just like yourselves. Of course the house wasn't run down then. Three years they lived here. Then, one morning the postman came with a parcel. He couldn't get any reply, so he left the parcel outside - nobody would steal anything in those days - but when he made a delivery the next day it was still there. He knew they hadn't gone away so he got suspicious. He went in the

Late Of This Address   **ACT II Scene 2**

back door and found them.

RICK: Dead?

CHARLOTTE: Both of them. Poisoned, I believe.

VICKY: Ugh! How horrible! I wish we'd known all this before we bought the place.

CHARLOTTE: The police came, but they never found anything. They put it down to a suicide pact.

RICK: Suicide...? Why?

CHARLOTTE: Search me. Probably because they couldn't find any evidence to the contrary.

VICKY: Perhaps they were right.

CHARLOTTE: I doubt it. Most locals thought he was a bit of a womaniser, and that she'd found out and killed him, then killed herself the same way.

VICKY: *(Looking nervously L)* That's terrible!

RICK: How d'you know all this?

CHARLOTTE: I told you... Local people and the papers. I've got *all* the press cuttings. I'm a bit of an amateur psychic, you see. This is the best house I've ever found. I'm *sure* the place is haunted. The older locals - those who were around at the time - won't come up here. And now *you've* seen them too.

VICKY: You say you've got all the cuttings?

CHARLOTTE: Yes. A whole scrapbook full.

VICKY: Could we see them?

CHARLOTTE: I suppose so. If you want. I'll tell you what... why don't you come down to the inn tonight and I'll bring them.

VICKY: Alright. We will.

RICK: Er... no. *(With meaning)* We can't go out tonight, Vicky!

VICKY: *(Puzzled)* Can't we?

RICK: *(Trying to remind her they are trapped in the house)* No, we *can't*, remember? We *have* to stay in.... We're.... expecting visitors!

VICKY: *(Realising)* Oh... Yes... I forgot.

RICK: Could you bring them here, d'you think?

CHARLOTTE: Yes, of course. I'll bring them in the morning if that's alright. About nine?

RICK: Yes, that's fine.

CHARLOTTE: *(Rising)* Then I'll be off.

VICKY: Charlotte, before you go....

CHARLOTTE: Yes?

VICKY: Have you ever actually *seen* a ghost?

Late Of This Address   **ACT II Scene 2**

CHARLOTTE: Sadly, no. Heard them, seen things move and so on, but... *(She shrugs.)*

VICKY: If you did, would you know how to get rid of her?

RICK: *Her?*

VICKY: *(Quickly)* Or him... Whichever.

CHARLOTTE: Well, not having had any actual practical experience, I can't be sure. But I've got plenty of books on the subject, so I could have a try. *(Moving towards the door R)* That's why I came back here... I lost the one I was hoping to use. It's a very rare one.... Rather unusual. *(She looks round the floor.)*

VICKY: We'll have a look round as we're clearing up. Maybe it'll turn up.

CHARLOTTE: *(She recreates her previous entry.)* Let's see... I came in here... And when I saw you I turned round, dropped my books here... So it should be... *(She spots the book under the sideboard.)* Ah, there we are! *(She retrieves the book.)* Marvellous what you can do when you put your mind to it. Retrace your steps and there you are!

VICKY: *(Feigning interest)* What exactly *is* the book?

CHARLOTTE: It's called "The Spirit World - The Paranormal Explained". It's by this chap called Walter Stein. Traditional spiritualists think he was a bit too radical in his thoughts.

VICKY: And you?

CHARLOTTE: I keep an open mind. I have had some small success with one or two of his methods. The odd incantation has bought some small responses.

VICKY: Would you mind if *I* borrowed it?

CHARLOTTE: *(Holding the book to her chest)* You?

VICKY: Yes... I'm quite interested. If we have to live in a haunted house I'd like to know what I'm dealing with.

CHARLOTTE: No, I'm afraid that's quite impossible!

VICKY: *(Surprised at her attitude)* Oh!

CHARLOTTE: I don't mean to be rude, but... Well, you mustn't dabble in things you don't understand, my dear. If you were to try some of the things in here and get them wrong.... Well, who knows the damage you could do?

RICK: *(Sotto voce)* I've got a fair idea!

CHARLOTTE: Pardon?

RICK: I said, er... "That's very fair, dear". *(To Vicky)* You don't want to cause any damage, do you, Vicky?

VICKY: Don't I?

CHARLOTTE: Believe me, you don't. I've heard cases of untrained people who have tried exorcisms and they've *never* got rid of the presence.

RICK: *Never!?*

Late Of This Address   ACT II Scene 2

CHARLOTTE: *Never!*
VICKY: In that case, you keep your book.
CHARLOTTE: Very wise, my dear... Very wise. And now I really must be off. I'll return in the morning.
VICKY: I'll see you out.
(VICKY moves towards the door R, then meets the invisible "barrier".)
VICKY: *(Returning C)* Actually, my husband will see you out.
CHARLOTTE: Until tomorrow, then.
VICKY: Tomorrow.
(CHARLOTTE exits R, followed by a wary RICK. The front door is heard to open off R, followed by polite "goodbyes" and the door closing again. RICK enters R.)
RICK: She was right.
VICKY: Charlotte?
RICK: No, Jessica. I tried to step out onto the drive, but I couldn't.
VICKY: What're we going to do?
RICK: I don't know yet. We'll just have to bide our time and see if there's anything we can do. We don't appear to be in any danger as long as we do what they say.
VICKY: This doesn't seem real. I'm not dreaming, am I?
RICK: I only wish you were. *(A pause.)* Why did you say you wanted to borrow her book?
VICKY: I was intrigued to know why she was so eager to get it back.
RICK: Well, it is hers...! Why did you hide it again?
VICKY: I didn't want her to know we'd seen it.
RICK: Why not?
VICKY: There's something funny about that book.
RICK: What makes you say that?
VICKY: I don't know. Just a feeling.
RICK: Is he here...? Ronnie?
VICKY: No... What about her....? Jessica?
RICK: No.
VICKY: D'you think they can hear us now?
RICK: I don't know. But I'm curious to know why they were in such a hurry to leave when Charlotte arrived.
VICKY: *She* might have been... *(She remembers Ronnie's kiss.)* He didn't seem at *all* bothered.
RICK: I wonder if they're scared of her.

44

Late Of This Address   **ACT II Scene 2**

VICKY: Who, Charlotte? Don't be ridiculous! She's a crank!

RICK: To you, maybe. But to a ghost...? Look what *you* managed to do by just reading one of her spells at random. *You* hadn't got a clue what you were doing, but *she* has. Imagine what she might be able to do to them.

VICKY: I wish we'd managed to hang on to that book. I could have had another go.

RICK: *(Down R)* I'm glad she took it.

VICKY: Why?

RICK: You tried to get rid of Jessica. All you managed to achieve was to reincarnate her husband!

VICKY: I'd have got the hang of it sooner or later.

RICK: By that time you'd probably have brought back their pet dog, cat and a couple of deceased goldfishes!

(JESSICA appears through the door L, leaving it open.)

VICKY: *(A hint of desperation)* There must be *something* we can do.

(RICK coughs and points to indicate that Jessica has returned.)

VICKY: *(To "Jessica")* So, you've come back at last, have you?

JESSICA: *(To Rick)* She's not very nice to me, is she? I get the impression she doesn't like me.

RICK: You could be right there.

VICKY: "Could be right"? What d'you mean... is she or isn't she?

RICK: Yes, she is... and I was talking to *her*!

JESSICA: Tell her my husband wants to speak to her.

RICK: Why, what does he want?

JESSICA: *I* don't know! I gave up trying to find out what *he* wants years ago!

VICKY: Rick... What is it? What's she saying?

RICK: *(Subconsciously leaning against the "barrier", giving the appearance of leaning on nothing)* Her husband wants you.

VICKY: Ronnie?

JESSICA: Oh, so we're on first name terms already, are we?

VICKY: What does he want?

RICK: She doesn't know.

VICKY: Why doesn't he come himself?

JESSICA: Oh, for God's sake, Ricky. Tell her to get out.

RICK: *(To Jessica)* Have a heart... She's frightened.

VICKY: I am not!

(JESSICA assumes a determined look and raises her hand towards Vicky. As VICKY tenses RICK stumbles and nearly falls as the "barrier" weakens. Sur-

Late Of This Address   **ACT II Scene 2**

prised, he looks R. VICKY *is being irresistibly drawn L.)*

VICKY: *(Starting to panic)* Rick! Help me!

RICK: *(Moving to Jessica)* What're you doing? Leave her alone.

(VICKY is now going through the open door L.)

JESSICA: *(Moving L; calling)* Ronnie... She's on her way. You take over. And behave yourself!

RONNIE: *(Off L, distant; calling)* O.K.

(VICKY gives a hopeless look to Rick and exits L. JESSICA makes a sweeping movement with her arm and the door L closes behind Vicky.)

VICKY: *(Off L; afraid)* Rick...!

(RICK looks at Jessica and then looks R. He makes a dash R.)

JESSICA: *(Turning and holding up her hand)* Stop!

(RICK freezes solid. JESSICA walks slowly to him.)

JESSICA: You didn't think I'd let you go that easily did you?

(JESSICA lowers her hand. RICK returns to normal.)

RICK: You can't blame me for trying.

JESSICA: *(Pensive)* No, perhaps not. Interesting that you were prepared to run off and leave the little woman, though.

RICK: What d'you mean?

JESSICA: Not very chivalrous, was it? You can't care about her that much.

RICK: Of course I do. She's my wife!

JESSICA: So? Ronnie's my husband, but I couldn't give a damn about *him*!

RICK: *(Adamant)* Well *I* care about Vicky!

JESSICA: Yet you were prepared to run off and leave her with Ronnie and me.

RICK: I was going for help.

JESSICA: *(Amused)* Help!? Who were you going to get?

RICK: I don't know. The police, I suppose.

JESSICA: And what were you going to tell them? That you've bought this house and it's got two ghosts in it!?

RICK: *I* don't know! It was a spur-of-the-moment thing!

JESSICA: *(Sitting on the settee)* Come and sit with me.

(RICK hesitates.)

JESSICA: *(Raising her hand)* I can make you if I want.

RICK: *(Going to her)* Alright, alright! *(He sits.)*

JESSICA: You just found out one of our weaknesses, didn't you?

RICK: *(Evasive)* I don't know what you mean!

JESSICA: Oh, come on, Ricky. You're not stupid. And nor am I.

Late Of This Address   ACT II Scene 2

RICK: Okay, okay. Yes, I think I have.
JESSICA: Well?
RICK: You can only control one of us at once, can't you?
JESSICA: Very good! *(A pause.)* Pity you didn't realise quicker. You could have been in the village by now.
RICK: What about Vicky?
JESSICA: Ronnie's looking after Vicky. He quite fancies her, you know.
RICK: *(Standing)* What's he doing to her?
JESSICA: *(An order)* Sit down!
   (RICK sits.)
RICK: *(More of a plea)* Please... What's he doing to her?
JESSICA: I don't know what he's doing to her. And, frankly, I don't care!
RICK: Aren't you jealous?
JESSICA: Of *him*!? With *her*!?
RICK: Yes. Surely you were happy once?
JESSICA: Once, maybe... But that was a *long* time ago.
RICK: What happened?
JESSICA: *(Firmly)* I don't want to talk about it!
RICK: It still hurts, then?
JESSICA: No, of course not! I couldn't give a damn!
RICK: *(Sarcastic)* Sounds like it!
JESSICA: If you must know, I got fed up with his succession of women.
   (RICK glances nervously off L.)
RICK: What went wrong?
JESSICA: *I* don't know. He used to travel a lot. He was in the record business.
RICK: Making them?
JESSICA: Selling them. He travelled round the country selling the latest hits to record shops. When he was away once he got a letter from one of them. A stupid little teenage typist. The stereotype dumb blonde. I asked him straight out as soon as he got back.
RICK: And?
JESSICA: He denied it, of course. *He* reckoned the letter came to the wrong address.
RICK: But *you* didn't?
JESSICA: Of course I didn't. I started remembering all the odd times when the telephone had rung with wrong numbers. They were obviously his women. He used to phone me from hotels, so I started to ring back. Several times he wasn't even registered!

Late Of This Address　　　　　　　　**ACT II Scene 3**

RICK: Why didn't you divorce him?

JESSICA: It wasn't as easy in those days. I kept confronting him about it and in the end he didn't even bother to deny it. We used to argue incessantly. *(Matter-of-fact)* Looking back, murder was the only answer.

RICK: *(Aghast)* Murder?

JESSICA: Yes.

RICK: You... you *killed* him!?

JESSICA: Me...!? No, of course not. I wish I *had*... *He* killed *me*!

RICK: I... I don't believe it!

JESSICA: It makes no difference whether you believe it or not. The evidence is before your eyes.

RICK: He actually *murdered* you?

JESSICA: That's right. Poison, the police said.

RICK: The police?

JESSICA: Yes. I actually watched my own murder investigation. Of course I wasn't able to tell anyone about it, so they never did find out what happened.

RICK: *(Dubious)* How did he poison you?

JESSICA: We were sleeping in separate rooms by then. He put this stuff on the doorknob, so the police said. I absorbed it through my skin.

RICK: You're very calm about it.

JESSICA: *(Matter-of-fact)* What can I do? I can hardly get my revenge, can I?

RICK: No, I suppose not. How did *he* die?

JESSICA: I'm not exactly sure about that. From what I could learn he was a bit sloppy and some of the poison got on *his* skin, too. Careless of him, eh?

RICK: And nobody found out what happened?

JESSICA: Not as far as I know.

RICK: That woman - Charlotte - said the Police believed it was a suicide pact.

JESSICA: Bumbling fools!

RICK: And the *locals*... *(He trails off.)*

JESSICA: What about them?

RICK: She said that popular opinion was that *you* found out about his women and poisoned him.

JESSICA: *(Amazed)* What!!?

RICK: Then you killed yourself out of remorse.

JESSICA: *(With dry amusement)* Hah! If I *had* killed the creep - which I didn't - remorse would *not* have been my emotion! The party'd still be going on!

RICK: But he killed you! Surely you feel bitter?

JESSICA: I did at first, but after a few years it wears off. Like I said... What's the point? The bitterness *I* feel isn't about him killing me. It's about the way he treated me when I was alive.

RICK: And...?

JESSICA: And now, thanks to your meddling, I have my chance of revenge.

RICK: But how?

JESSICA: Sauce for the goose, Ricky.

(JESSICA leans across an unresisting Rick and kisses him passionately.)

The CURTAIN falls

ACT II Scene 3

Evening the same day. The scene is unchanged. VICKY sits on the settee. RONNIE is pacing the room.

RONNIE: *(Spitting fire)* The absolute bitch! The rotten cow!

VICKY: *(Bitter)* You took the words right out of my mouth. And don't forget my pig of a husband!

RONNIE: I couldn't care less about *him*!

VICKY: Neither could I!

RONNIE: *(Coming to her)* How long have you been married?

VICKY: Six weeks.

RONNIE: Take my advice. Get out while you can.

VICKY: If only I'd known what he'd be like before I said "Yes".

RONNIE: We all change.

VICKY: *(Becoming tearful)* But this is so sudden. And it wouldn't be so bad if it was someone I could see! What am I going to tell all my friends...? "My husband's left me. He's run off with a ghost"! I could kill him! Honestly I could!

RONNIE: That's the last thing you want to do.

VICKY: *(Sobbing)* Why?

RONNIE: Because then they'd be together! *(After a pause. He sits next to her.)* Unless you.... *(He trails off.)*

VICKY: What?

RONNIE: *(Pensive)* No.... nothing...

VICKY: I've never seen him like this with a woman. Is she very attractive or something?

RONNIE: *(Lying)* No. Very plain. I can't think what I ever saw in her.

VICKY: When did *your* marriage start to go wrong?

RONNIE: Almost straight away. About the same as yours.

VICKY: What happened?

RONNIE: She didn't like me travelling. I was a salesman for a record company, so I had to go all over the country. She imagined I had a girl in every town.

VICKY: And did you?

RONNIE: *(Insulted)* Vicky! Do I look like the sort of bloke who'd cheat on his wife?

VICKY: *(Glancing off R)* Don't ask me! I obviously can't tell the difference!

RONNIE: That's anger talking. Look at me.

(VICKY looks into his eyes and is drawn by them.)

RONNIE: *(Taking her hands in his)* Tell me honestly. Is that the way you think I'd behave?

VICKY: *(Transfixed)* No.

RONNIE: *(Breaking the gaze)* I was innocent.

(VICKY returns to normality.)

RONNIE: I wouldn't mind, but I'd phone her every night. I ask you, would a cheating husband bother to do that?

VICKY: No, I suppose not.

RONNIE: She used to phone back and check up on me. She claimed that every so often she'd get no reply, or that the hotel would deny all knowledge of me. Between you and me I think she lost touch with reality. D'you know what she did once?

VICKY: What?

RONNIE: She wrote a letter to me, supposedly from one of my many girlfriends. She even sprayed it with perfume! Then she posted it to me - here - ready to challenge me when I came back! Mad.

VICKY: What did you do?

RONNIE: I told her not to be so bloody stupid! I mean, it was so obvious. For a start, the letter was typed.

VICKY: So?

RONNIE: What sort of girlfriend would type a love letter?

VICKY: Some might. A typist, maybe.

RONNIE: That's what *she* said. But the thing had been posted in the village! Not only that, but the perfume she used was one I'd bought her for her birthday just before we married.

VICKY: What did you do?

Late Of This Address   ACT II Scene 3

RONNIE: What *could* I do...? Maybe I should have tried harder to make it work, but I was under a lot of pressure. In the end she went and slept in the back bedroom. The only time we ever spoke to each other was when she accused me of my latest *supposed* affair. I gave up denying it in the end. Stupid of me, I suppose, but I never thought she'd stoop to murder.

VICKY: *(After an unbelieving pause)* What did you say?

RONNIE: Which bit?

VICKY: I could have sworn you said *"murder"*.

RONNIE: Yes, that's right.

VICKY: Are you saying she killed you?

RONNIE: *(Matter-of-fact)* Yes. Didn't you know?

VICKY: No, I didn't.

RONNIE: She poisoned me. God knows how. I never used to eat at home.

VICKY: And what happened to *her*?

RONNIE: I haven't a clue. I don't remember anything until you brought me back.

VICKY: Nothing at all?

RONNIE: Not a thing.

(VICKY is once again transfixed by Ronnie's stare. He takes her hands in his again.)

RONNIE: *(After a pause)* I'm very grateful, you know.

VICKY: *(Dreamy)* Are you?

RONNIE: Very.

VICKY: Good..... What for?

RONNIE: For bringing me back. *(A pause.)* Are you glad?

VICKY: What?

RONNIE: Are you glad I'm back?

VICKY: Oh.., yes.

RONNIE: And Rick?

VICKY: *(Lost in a trance)* Who?

RONNIE: *(Delighted with the power he has; breaking the gaze)* Rick... Your husband.

VICKY: Oh, him.... *(More normal)* You don't like him, do you?

RONNIE: He's alright. I'm just jealous, that's all.

VICKY: Jealous?

RONNIE: Yes. I wish Jessica had been like you.

VICKY: Do you?

RONNIE: Yes... *You* understand.

Late Of This Address   **ACT II Scene 3**

VICKY: *(She glances at her watch. Rising and moving R)* Where *are* they?

RONNIE: What does it matter?

VICKY: This is insane! I can't believe it. My own husband has gone out on a picnic with a ghost!

RONNIE: We can go out as well, if you want.

VICKY: *(Reacting)* I don't want...! *(Calmer)* I don't know *what* I want.

RONNIE: They'll be back soon. *(He pats the sofa next to him.)* Come and sit down.

VICKY: I don't want to sit down.

RONNIE: *(Firmer)* Vicky! *(Persuasive)* Look at me.

(VICKY reluctantly allows herself to be captured by his gaze again.)

RONNIE: Good. Now, come and sit with me.

(VICKY slowly goes and sits next to him.)

RONNIE: That dress is far too long.

VICKY: It's the fashion.

RONNIE: I don't like it. I bet you've got nice legs, too... Show me.

VICKY: What!?

RONNIE: Show me your legs.

VICKY: No! It's not right!

RONNIE: You know you can't resist me. Can you?

VICKY: *(Transfixed again)* No.

RONNIE: Then show me your legs.

(VICKY, transfixed, raises her hem to her knees.)

RONNIE: Very nice. A bit higher.

(VICKY raises her hem slightly above her knees. RONNIE'S eyes widen.)

RONNIE: *(His hand moving to her knee)* Beautiful.

(RONNIE leans across to kiss her. VICKY does not resist. The door R opens suddenly. JESSICA and RICK enter. JESSICA takes in the scene and is furious.)

JESSICA: Ronnie! You bastard. Leave her alone!

(RONNIE breaks from VICKY, who returns to normality. As JESSICA advances on him, RONNIE rises and backs off L.)

RONNIE: Trust you, Jessie! You always did arrive at the wrong time!

JESSICA: I'll give you wrong time! Twenty years in hell haven't changed you a bit, have they!?

RONNIE: Being in hell isn't much different from living with you!

(RONNIE exits L, followed by an irate JESSICA, leaving VICKY and RICK staring at each other incredulously.)

Late Of This Address   **ACT II Scene 3**

RICK: *(Accusing)* What were you doing!?
VICKY: Why should *you* care!?
RICK: You're my wife. Or had you forgotten!?
VICKY: Yes! Why did you have to spoil it by reminding me!?
RICK: It beats me what I ever saw in you!
VICKY: It beats me what *she* sees in you!
RICK: At least she doesn't sit around with her skirt round her neck!
VICKY: *(Tugging her hem down)* So *you* say! *I* can't see her, so I wouldn't know! *(A short pause.)* I bet she's got lousy legs anyway!
RICK: She's got gorgeous legs. *(Taunting)* And the extremely short mini-dress she wears show them off to perfection!
VICKY: Now I *know* you've flipped. Ronnie says she's plain!
RICK: Ronnie would!
VICKY: At least *he* knows how to treat a girl!
RICK: I should think so! From what Jessica tells me he's had plenty of practice!
VICKY: He told me about that, too. She *imagined* he had loads of girlfriends. That's why she killed him!
RICK: *Jessica* said that... *(He is about to continue the argument when he realises what she has said)* What did you say?
VICKY: *(Surprised at his sudden change of mood)* I said she imagined he had loads of girlfriends. That's why she killed him.... Why?
RICK: D'you believe him?
VICKY: *(Firmly)* Yes, I do! *(After a pause)* Why?
RICK: Because Jessica told me that *he* killed *her*.
VICKY: *(More curious)* And *you* believe *her*?
RICK: *(Pensive)* Yes, I do. Which means... *(He trails off in thought.)*
VICKY: *(Venomous again)* Which means *she's* a liar!
RICK: Or *he* is!
(The idea dawns on both of them at the same time.)
Or...
VICKY: *(Together)* Someone else did it!
RICK:
VICKY: D'you really think...!?
RICK: It's possible!
VICKY: And they each think the other one killed them.
RICK: But who..? Who could have done it?
VICKY: There's no way *we* could know that. It could have been anyone. And whoever it was has probably moved away years ago.

Late Of This Address   ACT II Scene 3

RICK: Or died themselves. *(A pause.)* We've got to tell them!
VICKY: Who, *them*?
RICK: Yes. Before they do each other a mischief.
VICKY: Is that possible?
(Right on cue, RONNIE backs in from the door L, followed by JESSICA. Her anger is unabated.)
JESSICA: ...And not content with having it off with every woman alive, you now have to start from the grave!
RONNIE: You've no room to talk! It was you who took the husband out for a picnic. Picnic! Hah!
JESSICA: Making love with you is probably the same now you're dead as it was when you were alive!
RICK: Er... Jessica. Excuse me, but...!
JESSICA: *(To Rick)* Stay out of this! *(To Ronnie)* I suppose you gave her the old "my wife doesn't understand me" routine!?
VICKY: Yes I did, as a matter of fact. It was the truth!
(VICKY and RICK silently count "one, two, three".)
JESSICA: Any woman who doesn't understand you must be a pea-brain!
RICK: *(Together, on "three"; shouting)* Will you shut up!?
VICKY:
JESSICA: *(Staring at them; together)* What!?
RONNIE:
VICKY: I know you can both hear me, so I'll speak to both of you. Ricky and I have just been having a little chat.
JESSICA: I bet!
RICK: *(To Jessica)* Shhh!
VICKY: It seems that you believe you were each murdered by the other. Yes?
JESSICA: *(Looking curiously at Ronnie)* What?
RONNIE: *(Looking curiously at Jessica)* Yes, I remember...
VICKY: We think we may have come up with another possibility.
JESSICA: *(After a pause; to Vicky)* Well?
RICK: *(Realising Vicky cannot hear Jessica)* Someone else did it. Murdered you both.
(JESSICA and RONNIE stare at each other.)
JESSICA: That's ridiculous!
RONNIE: No, Jessie, wait! It's just possible.
VICKY: Have you any idea of who it could have been?
JESSICA: *(To Ronnie)* One of your many paramours..., *(sarcastic)* darling!

Late Of This Address   ACT II Scene 3

RONNIE: Jessie, if I've told you once I've told you a hundred times...
JESSICA: And I *still* don't believe you!
VICKY: Time to come clean, Ronnie!
RONNIE: What d'you mean?
RICK: *(To Vicky)* What did he say?
VICKY: *(To Rick)* Shhh! *(To Ronnie)* You're wife may not have understood you, but *I* do!
RONNIE: You do?
VICKY: Times have changed, Ronnie. Women are much more aware these days. Trying to undress somebody else's wife in broad daylight when her husband and your wife are due back any minute is *not* the way a devoted husband behaves.
RICK: He did *what*!? *(Looking wildly about; threatening)* Where is he?
RONNIE: I never said I was devoted...
JESSICA: *(Amused)* Hah! She's not as stupid as I thought! She's obviously got you sussed!
RONNIE: Jessie... It's not true! I....
VICKY: You might as well admit it, Ronnie. The harm was done twenty years ago.
RICK: *(To Vicky)* Vicky! Will you *please* tell me what's going on!?
VICKY: In a minute. Be patient!
RONNIE: *(Defeated)* O.K. I suppose you're right. *(Genuinely sorry)* I'm sorry, Jessie.
JESSICA: I almost believe you mean that.
RICK: Mean what?
RONNIE: I do. Really I do.
JESSICA: But why, Ronnie? What did I do wrong?
RONNIE: It wasn't you, it was me. I never grew up. Being in the record business it was dead easy. They were the days of free love and the permissive society. I was like a kid in a sweet shop.
JESSICA: And it cost us both our lives!
VICKY: Have you any idea who might have wanted you dead?
JESSICA: Judging by what I've just heard it could have been half the teenagers of England!
RONNIE: But why *me*?
JESSICA: *(As if a line from a melodrama)* Perhaps one of the sweet little things couldn't do without you. "If I can't have him, nobody will!"
VICKY: We'll help you.

RICK: We'll help them what?

VICKY: Find out who the murderer was.

RICK: *(Incredulous)* How are we going to do that? We were only kids when all this happened!

VICKY: So?

RICK: Vicky...! We already agreed that whoever it was is probably either dead or moved away.

VICKY: We could talk to the locals. Somebody must have seen something.

RICK: Charlotte already did that. The locals believe it was a suicide pact or that they killed each other. If someone else had been involved *someone* would have said *something*!

VICKY: *(To Ronnie)* Could you give us a list of all your friends and acquaintances? *And* your girlfriends?

JESSICA: Yes... What did you do with your little black book, Ronnie!?

RONNIE: I never *had* a little black book...! But yes, we could make up a list.

JESSICA: *(Reluctantly)* Yes, alright. I'll make a list, too.

RICK: This is ridiculous! They'll never be able to remember all their acquaintances after twenty years!

VICKY: It's *not* twenty years to them. It's like it was yesterday.

RICK: *(To Jessica)* Is that right?

JESSICA: I'm afraid so. I'm an old woman, really. Except that I never got any older.

RICK: If we do have a list, how are we going to eliminate people?

VICKY: Perhaps Jessica and Ronnie can do some research of those who have died?

RONNIE: No use asking me. I wouldn't know where to start. I've not been back long enough, so I've still to learn the tools of the trade.

JESSICA: Nor me.

VICKY: *(To Rick)* What about Jessica?

(RICK shakes his head.)

VICKY: Wonderful. Charlotte spends all her days trying to speak to the dead and they can't even do it themselves!

RICK: That's it! Charlotte! *She* can try! She's coming round in the morning with those press cuttings.

JESSICA: Ridiculous! She's a charlatan!

RICK: It's worth a try! Unless you have any better ideas?

(JESSICA reluctantly shakes her head.)

JESSICA: One condition. *I* don't want to be in the room when she tries. It

Late Of This Address   **ACT III**

frightens the life out of me.
RONNIE: We're only talking about twenty years ago. Chances are whoever it was is still alive. Especially if it *was* one of my *(sheepish)* girlfriends.
VICKY: Just make the list. Rick and I can start to research the living. We can start with the locals and gradually work wider.
RICK: We'd have to find proof.
VICKY: Let's worry about that when we find the killer. Come on... let's get some sleep.
(VICKY takes Rick's hand and they exit L. JESSICA and RONNIE look at each other for a few moments.)
JESSICA: *(Holding out her hand; forgiving)* Come on, superstud. It looks like we're in the spare room!
(JESSICA leads Ronnie off L as the CURTAIN falls.)

ACT III

The following morning. The room has been significantly tidied. JESSICA and VICKY are just putting the finishing touches to arranging the furniture. At one point JESSICA has to move quickly aside to prevent VICKY from walking into her. RICK enters L, wearing an apron.

JESSICA: *(To Jessica; seeing Rick's apron)* And to think I fancied him!
RICK: Any sign of her?
VICKY: Not yet. Take that apron off. You look stupid.
RICK: *(Taking off the apron)* Where's Ronnie?
VICKY: No idea. Where's Jessica?
RICK: Standing next to you.
VICKY: It's been quite an experience tidying up while seeing cushions and ornaments apparently floating through the air!
JESSICA: *(To Vicky)* You should worry! *(She turns to Rick.)* I wish you'd tell her to watch where she's walking.
RICK: Now don't you two start bickering again! If I hadn't seen it with my own eyes I'd never have believed two women could have an argument when one of them can't even see the other!
VICKY: What's she been saying?
RICK: Nothing... She just says she wishes you'd watch where you're going.

Late Of This Address   **ACT III**

VICKY: I do. I avoid everything I can see. Maybe if she could carry something around I could avoid *her*!

JESSICA: Tell her to stop talking about me as if I'm not here!

RICK: It's an idea, Jessica. If you could carry something visible, and so could Ronnie, we'd know where you were. *(He picks up a large ornament and offers it to her.)* Here. Try this.

JESSICA: If you think I'm walking around carrying *that* all day you can think again! Of all the bloody stupid ideas!

VICKY: What did she say?

RICK: She wasn't very keen on the idea.

JESSICA: *(Shouting at Vicky)* I said it was a bloody stupid idea!

VICKY: Is she shouting at me!?

RICK: How on earth did you know that?

VICKY: Women's intuition. Tell her to go to hell!

RICK: Will you two please behave!? We're supposed to be working together to find the killer, remember? Now, Vicky, say sorry to Jessica.

VICKY: *(Reluctantly; talking to a point well away from Jessica)* I'm sorry.

RICK: That's better. Now, Jessica. Say you're sorry to Vicky.

JESSICA: Get stuffed!

VICKY: Tell her I accept her apology.

RICK: You can tell her yourself, remember?

VICKY: I'd rather *you* told her.

RICK: *(Defeated)* Very well. Jessica, Vicky accepts your apology.

JESSICA: I didn't apologise! I've nothing to be sorry for.

RICK: *(To Vicky)* Jessica accepts *your* apology too.

(There is a knock at the door off R.)

VICKY: That'll be Charlotte. *(She exits R.)*

JESSICA: Time for me to depart.

RICK: You can stay if you want.

JESSICA: No thanks. I told you.... Psychics give me the creeps.

RICK: What about Ronnie?

JESSICA: *(Firmly)* He can stay with me.

(The front door is heard to open off R.)

CHARLOTTE: *(Hearty)* Good morning, good morning! And how are we today?

VICKY: *(Off R)* Fine. Here, let me take you coat.

CHARLOTTE: Thanks. Bitterly cold this morning.

(CHARLOTTE enters R. She is removing a scarf as she enters. She carries a

Late Of This Address   **ACT III**

battered folder containing newspaper cuttings.)
RICK: Morning, Charlotte. Thanks for coming. Please... sit down.
(CHARLOTTE sits on the settee. RICK sits next to her.)
VICKY: Would you like a coffee?
CHARLOTTE: Oh, yes, dear. Please. Anything to keep out the chill.
VICKY: I'll go and make you one. How d'you like it?
CHARLOTTE: Strong, please. No milk or sugar.
VICKY: Rick?
RICK: Please.
VICKY: *(As she exits L)* Don't start without me.
(VICKY exits L, closing the door. A short time later - far too soon to have made any coffee - she returns with a tray containing three hot cups of coffee, which she hands out. She leaves the door open. RICK looks puzzled.)
CHARLOTTE: *(Surprised)* Thank you. That was quick.
RICK: Er... It's instant coffee!
VICKY: *(Giving him a look)* I er... I had the kettle on when you arrived. I only had to pour it.
(CHARLOTTE takes her coffee and sips. RICK looks quizzically at VICKY, who - unseen by Charlotte - signals by mouthing words and pointing with her hands - that Jessica had made the coffee.)
CHARLOTTE: Lovely.
VICKY: Did you bring the newspaper cuttings?
CHARLOTTE: *(Tapping her folder)* All in here.
(VICKY sits on the arm of the settee next to Charlotte, who opens the folder and shows them the cuttings.)
CHARLOTTE: *(Indicating one of the cuttings)* This was one from the "Daily Express". The nationals were very keen for a couple of days, but they soon lost interest. *(Pointing)* That one's the husband, Ronald. This was the wife, Jessica.
VICKY: *(Looking close)* Hmmm! She's *very* attractive. *(Staring daggers at Rick)* Not at *all* plain!
(RICK looks sheepish.)
CHARLOTTE: No. They were both quite good looking.... *(A slight pause.)* Judging from the photographs.
RICK: *(Pointedly to Vicky)* Yes. *He* looks quite good... in a flash sort of way, of course.
VICKY: Yes. I can understand why women found him attractive.
CHARLOTTE: Sad, really. His attraction was part of his downfall. *(She turns*

59

Late Of This Address   **ACT III**

---

to another cutting.) This is from one of the local papers. It's closed down now, but I managed to get these from their archives. This is the police inspector in charge of the case. Dreadful man, by all accounts. Bumbling and incompetent. He's the one who came up with the suicide pact idea.

VICKY: Have you spoken to him?

CHARLOTTE: No... He's dead now.

VICKY: You don't sound as though you agree with the suicide pact theory.

CHARLOTTE: I don't.

RICK: Why not?

CHARLOTTE: Well, he's supposed to have had all these girlfriends..., yes?

RICK: Yes.

CHARLOTTE: None of whom ever came forward.

VICKY: I don't see what....

CHARLOTTE: *(Interrupting)* Which casts doubt on whether there actually *were* any girlfriends in the first place. Despite that, it was troubled marriage.

VICKY: How d'you know?

CHARLOTTE: I've spoken to everyone I can find who knew them. I do assure you, it definitely was *not* a happy marriage. After the first flush, that is. I am forced to conclude, therefore, that it is unlikely that two such disparate souls would enter into *any* sort of pact, let alone for suicide.

RICK: *(After consideration)* Sounds reasonable.

CHARLOTTE: Accepting that, added to the lack of any evidence of his *supposed* girlfriends, leads me to believe that she killed him, purely because she *imagined* he was unfaithful to her.

RICK: And who killed her?

CHARLOTTE: There I'm not so certain. It's probable that she killed herself, though whether it was out of remorse or fear of capture, or possibly even by accident, remains a mystery and will probably remain a mystery for all time.

RICK: *(To Vicky)* That all sounds very plausible.

VICKY: Yes.

(While CHARLOTTE is engrossed in her folder, VICKY and RICK exchange nervous glances, and both look warily to off L. Suddenly JESSICA bursts in.)

JESSICA: That's absolute rubbish! I didn't kill him! She's got it all wrong!

CHARLOTTE: *(Picking up her coffee)* Brrrh! Dreadfully cold this morning.

(Unseen by Charlotte, RICK glares at Jessica and indicates by waving his arms that she should leave.)

JESSICA: Alright, I'll go. But I'll be listening. She's got it all wrong. *(She exits L.)*

RICK: *(Unthinking)* Sorry about that.

CHARLOTTE: *(Puzzled)* Sorry about what?

RICK: *(Realising what he has said; quickly)* The cold. I er... I should have turned the heating up.

CHARLOTTE: No matter. *(Showing them a glossy photograph)* This was taken at the funeral.

VICKY: Where did you get that?

CHARLOTTE: Mr Shorter, the chap who used to take photographs for the local papers used to run a photography business in the village. He's retired now, but he let me rummage through all his old photographs in his attic.

VICKY: How d'you know it was from their funeral - Jessica and Ronnie's? It could be anyone's.

CHARLOTTE: *(Turning the photograph over)* It's written on the back. Mr Shorter was very meticulous.

VICKY: *(Studying the photograph)* Who are all these people?

CHARLOTTE: Well... those are *his* parents. That's his brother and family. These are *her* parents and her two sisters.

VICKY: What about these?

CHARLOTTE: That one was some chap he worked with, and that woman was her best friend - a bridesmaid at their wedding, I believe.

VICKY: And these three?

CHARLOTTE: No idea, I'm afraid. As you can see their faces are not exactly clear. I've tried everything I know to trace them, but, alas.... *(She trails off.)*

VICKY: They could be the missing girlfriends.

CHARLOTTE: Possibly, but I doubt it. As I said.... every line of enquiry has drawn a blank on his girlfriends, and they'd hardly be likely to turn up at the funeral.

RICK: No... Perhaps you're right.

CHARLOTTE: *(She closes her folder.)* And that's about it, I'm afraid. The others are very much the same thing. You're welcome to borrow them if you wish, as long as I get them back.

RICK: Yes, thanks. We'll get them back to you, don't worry.

VICKY: You believe this house is haunted, don't you?

CHARLOTTE: Oh, yes! That's why I've spent the last few years here.

VICKY: I presume you believe it's the dead couple who haunt the place?

CHARLOTTE: Possibly both... Maybe just one.

VICKY: What exactly have you seen here?

CHARLOTTE: Not a great deal in the spiritual sense. I mean, lights come on and off on their own, and there are always bangs and crashes, but that's not particularly unusual. I've experienced many houses where that sort of thing

Late Of This Address   ACT III

goes on.

RICK: So what draws you to *this* house particularly?

CHARLOTTE: Well, young man... there's something about this house. An atmosphere. Something that's difficult to explain to the uninitiated. *(A pause.)* Unless, of course you've experienced it?

VICKY: No, no. Nothing. Have we, Rick?

RICK: Not a thing.

CHARLOTTE: There you are, you see. But *I* have. Sometimes it's just like a cold breeze, but the air is quite still. Sometimes it's an almost overpowering warmth. But it's there alright. I know it is.

VICKY: Have you ever tried to exorcise it?

CHARLOTTE: Good heavens, no, my dear! I don't want it to go away! I want to bring it back! I want to see it, talk to it! There's so much to be learned!

VICKY: What about a séance? Have you ever tried that?

CHARLOTTE: No, I have not. For a séance you need at least three people, and I'm afraid the locals tolerate my er... *eccentricity* rather than co-operate with it.

VICKY: *We* could do it with you.

RICK: Vicky!

VICKY: We could. It's our house, so it's only proper that we should.

CHARLOTTE: I couldn't ask you... Could I?

VICKY: Yes.... Please... We want to. Don't we, Rick? *(No reply. Firmer)* Don't we, Rick?

RICK: Yes, I suppose so.

CHARLOTTE: Very well. We'll do it!

VICKY: *(Standing)* What do we need?

CHARLOTTE: We'll need some lettered cards - I have some in my car - and a glass.

(VICKY gets a glass from the sideboard and gives it to Charlotte.)

CHARLOTTE: Perhaps you could move that table under the light. I'll get the cards.

(CHARLOTTE dashes excitedly off R, while RICK organises the table into stage C.)

VICKY: You said she was plain!

RICK: Who?

VICKY: Jessica!

RICK: So?

VICKY: She doesn't exactly *look* plain! You lied to me.

62

Late Of This Address   ACT III

RICK: So? You'd only have worried?
(CHARLOTTE enters R.)
VICKY: *(As Charlotte enters)* Worried!?
RICK: Shhh!
(VICKY helps Rick arrange the chairs. CHARLOTTE sits above C of the table and carefully arranges the cards across the table to form an alphabet.)
RICK: I don't believe it! A Ouija board!
CHARLOTTE: You may scoff, young man, but it can be very effective. Now, if you'll sit either side of me.... *(To Vicky)* You sit here, my dear.
(VICKY sits L and RICK sits R of the table CHARLOTTE places the upturned glass on the table in front of her.)
RICK: Shouldn't we have the lights dimmed or something?
CHARLOTTE: Whatever for? Now... if you'll both put the index finger of your right hand on top of the glass next to mine...
(VICKY does so. RICK does not.)
VICKY: Come on, Rick.
(RICK reluctantly does as he is bid. His left hand is in his lap.)
CHARLOTTE: *(Closing her eyes)* Now..., concentrate.
RICK: What on?
VICKY: Rick! *(She closes her eyes.)*
CHARLOTTE: *(Grandly)* Is there anybody there...? Is there anybody there...?
JESSICA: *(Peering through the door L)* Of course there bloody-well is! You already know that!
CHARLOTTE: *(Stiffening in her seat)* Yes...! Yes...! I can feel something!
JESSICA: *(Teasing)* Rick...! Both hands on the table, please!
(RICK glares at Jessica. JESSICA enters the room, stands behind Rick and ruffles his hair.)
VICKY: *(To Charlotte)* What is it?
CHARLOTTE: Can't you feel it...? The... the presence?
(JESSICA is now rubbing her hands down Rick's chest.)
VICKY: I can't feel a thing.
RICK: *(Hoarse)* I'm beginning to feel something.
JESSICA: Naughty, naughty!
CHARLOTTE: *(Getting carried away)* Good! Excellent! We're getting through! Who is there...? *(Nothing.)* Tell us... who is there?
VICKY: Nothing's happening.
CHARLOTTE: Patience, my dear. Patience. Can you hear me? Who is trying to get through?

Late Of This Address   **ACT III**

JESSICA: *(Losing patience)* Oh, for God's sake, let's put the silly cow out of her misery.
(To the amazement of Vicky and Charlotte, JESSICA takes hold of the glass and starts to move it to spell out her name. CHARLOTTE's and VICKY's eyes open wide.)

VICKY: *(Watching the glass)* J.... E.... S.... S.... Jessica!

CHARLOTTE: *(Breaking her hold on the glass)* It's her! It's the wife!

JESSICA: Hooray! Go to the top of the class!

VICKY: *(Suspicious)* Rick...! Did *you* do that!?

RICK: No, Vicky...! She's here... *(Correcting himself)* That is... I *think* she's really here!

CHARLOTTE: *(To Rick; excited)* It's you! She's communicating through you!

VICKY: *(Sotto voce)* I'd never have guessed!

CHARLOTTE: Now what do we do?

RICK: *I* don't know.... You're the psychic!

JESSICA: This is a waste of time, Ricky! *She* might think she's made some major breakthrough, but we're no further on than we were last night.

VICKY: Why don't you see if we can communicate with the husband?

CHARLOTTE: I'll give it a try. *(To Rick)* Keep concentrating on the wife. Don't let her go.

JESSICA: *(Sliding between Rick and the table and sitting on his knee)* Don't worry. I've no intention of going anywhere.

CHARLOTTE: *(Noticing the movement of the table)* Her presence is *very* powerful. Did you feel that?

RICK: *(As Jessica squirms on his lap)* Oh, yes. I felt it alright.

VICKY: *(Realising what Jessica might be up to; impatient)* What about the husband?

CHARLOTTE: All in good time. *(Excited)* Oh, this is wonderful...! Wonderful! Now, my dears... Fingers on the glass.
(They all put their fingers on the glass again.)

CHARLOTTE: *(Her eyes closed; dramatically)* Is there anyone *else* there...? We want to speak to Ronald.... Is Ronald there....?

JESSICA: *(Calling to off L, matter-of-fact)* Ronnie...! You're wanted!

RONNIE: *(Off L)* Is it safe?

JESSICA: Of course it's safe. The old bat's completely mad!
(RONNIE enters L. VICKY notices his arrival. RONNIE takes in the scene.)

RONNIE: Leave him alone, Jessie. He's married.

VICKY: *(To Ronnie; without thinking)* What's she doing?

CHARLOTTE: *(Her eyes snapping open)* What's who doing?

(VICKY realises what she has said and quickly assumes a state of trance.)

VICKY: *(In a deep, ghostly "male" voice)* My wife... What's she doing?

CHARLOTTE: *(Excitedly to Rick)* Oh, this is marvellous! The husband's communicating through your wife.

JESSICA: Oh, it's pathetic!

RONNIE: We agreed to give it a try, Jessie.

JESSICA: I know we did, but it's a total waste of time.

RONNIE: Not necessarily. *(To Vicky)* See if she can raise anyone else.

JESSICA: Like who?

RONNIE: Like our *killer*, Jessie.. That's what we're here for isn't it? *(To Vicky)* Pretend you're me.

(VICKY speaks as if entranced, much to Rick's amazement.)

VICKY: I want to find my killer!

CHARLOTTE: *(Taken aback)* What?

VICKY: I want to find my killer!

CHARLOTTE: This can't be happening! If this is some sort of joke....

RICK: It's no joke... That's not Vicky talking.

CHARLOTTE: *(Nervously)* Is that really Ronald?

VICKY: Yes. I want to find my killer.

CHARLOTTE: But... but your wife killed you.... It was in all the papers.

JESSICA: *(To Ronnie)* Tell her I didn't do it.

RONNIE: *(To Vicky)* Tell her Jessie didn't do it.

JESSICA: *(To Rick)* You tell her!

RICK: *(Assuming a similar - but "female" - mystical voice to imitate Jessica)* I didn't do it!

VICKY: No! Jessica did not kill me.

JESSICA: Tell her someone killed us both.

RICK: No. Somebody killed me, too! Both of us!

(CHARLOTTE rises suddenly, causing the cards to tip off the table. She backs away from them. RICK and VICKY are amazed at her attitude and drop any pretence of trances.)

CHARLOTTE: *(In horror)* No..! It's not true...! *(To Vicky)* She did it! Jessica! You must believe me! *She* did it!

JESSICA: *(Mystified; in her normal voice)* What the hell's come over her?

RONNIE: *(Going over to the cowering Charlotte)* Wait a minute! I *know* her! It's not Charlotte.... It's... *(Searching his memory)* It's.... Tracy!

JESSICA: Who the hell's Tracy?

Late Of This Address　　　　　　　　　　**ACT III**

RONNIE: She was a typist I knew in Manchester. Tracy Black.

JESSICA: One of your nonexistent girlfriends?

RONNIE: Yes. *(To Charlotte)* Tracy... is that you?

RICK: What shall we do?

RONNIE: *(Realising)* Of course! She wanted me to leave you. She wanted to marry me. She must be the killer!

VICKY: *(Assuming the entranced voice again)* You are not Charlotte.... You are Tracy Black!

CHARLOTTE: *(Wailing)* No...! No!

VICKY: Tracy Black! Our killer!

CHARLOTTE: *(Pleading to Vicky)* I didn't mean it, Ronnie! *(Indicating Rick)* It was *her* I was after. If she was dead we could have been together! That's all I wanted! I'm sorry! I'm so sorry!

JESSICA: I almost feel sorry for her. Almost.

(VICKY takes a sobbing Charlotte and sits with her on the settee. All pretence of the séance has now gone.)

VICKY: Why did you do it?

CHARLOTTE: I loved him. I really did. I'd have done anything for him, *anything*. But he wouldn't divorce her. In the end I gave him an ultimatum... her or me. He said he didn't really love *me*, he really loved *her*. So I killed her. It seemed so simple. The only way out. Except it all went wrong.

JESSICA: The bitch! Ask her how.

RICK: How did you do it?

CHARLOTTE: My brother was a scientist with some secret government place in the Lake District. He got me the poison. It was what they call a contact poison. It's absorbed through the skin and the effects are almost immediate. I'd arranged to meet Ronnie in Manchester so I knew he wouldn't be at home, then I travelled down here. I put some poison on the milk bottle on the front step in the morning. And I watched and waited. I saw her come out and pick the bottles up. It was perfect.

RONNIE: Except that I never went to Manchester.

CHARLOTTE: When I was sure she'd touched the bottle I got the fast train back to Manchester to meet Ronnie. The perfect alibi. Except that he never arrived. He was here all the time. *(To Vicky)* Why didn't you go, Ronnie? Why!?

JESSICA: Yes, Ronnie... Why didn't you go?

RONNIE: I was going to. I'd packed my bags and everything. The irony of all this is that just as I was about to leave I realised what a pillock I was being - galavanting round the country chasing after girls like a teenager. I'd decided

Late Of This Address ACT III

I'd been an absolute bastard and I was determined to make it up to you. I made a resolution there and then - no more women. I loved you when I married you and I realised I still did. I thought we could spend the rest of our life together.

JESSICA: We did that alright! About eight hours of it!

RONNIE: It's not fair!

CHARLOTTE: Can you *really* speak to them?

VICKY: Yes. Jessica appeared to Rick soon after we arrived. Then when you left that book here I had a go at getting rid of her and I conjured up Ronnie.

CHARLOTTE: Can you see them?

RICK: *I* can see Jessica and Vicky can see Ronnie.

CHARLOTTE: But not the other way round?

RICK: No.

CHARLOTTE: And between you you set me up.

VICKY: We never meant to. We had no idea it was you. We didn't know *who* it was.

RICK: We just thought that maybe the official verdict was wrong. We wanted you to try to contact people who might have known more... The killer even!

CHARLOTTE: You did *that* alright. *(A pause.)* Can they hear me?

VICKY: Every word.

CHARLOTTE: Where are they now?

VICKY: *(Indicating where Ronnie is standing)* Ronnie's here...

RICK: *(Indicating where Jessica is standing)* And Jessica's over here.

CHARLOTTE: *(Advancing on Jessica's position)* Jessica, I'm so terribly sorry. I was a love-struck teenager. I didn't know what I was doing.

JESSICA: *(Moving away)* Keep her away from me!

RICK: So all this psychic stuff is just a front?

CHARLOTTE: Oh, no. I really *am* a psychic. I first noticed it at the funeral. I was standing there and...

VICKY: *(Interrupting)* You were there?

CHARLOTTE: Yes. I was one of the three in the photograph. Thankfully the police didn't trace me.

RONNIE: Why, of all the bloody nerve! She kills us and then comes to the funeral!

CHARLOTTE: I had to be close to him one last time. And when I was standing in that cemetery it was deafening. Voices, hundreds of them, all from beyond. From that day forward I've been trying to make contact with Ronnie. I had to make him understand. I need his forgiveness. *(Looking towards where she thinks Ronnie is; pleading)* Tell me you forgive me, Ronnie!

67

RONNIE: Like hell I do!

JESSICA: And if it matters at all, *I* don't either!

CHARLOTTE: Did he say anything?

VICKY: Yes, but not what you wanted to hear.

RICK: *(Suddenly; looking round)* Jessica...!? *(To Vicky)* Vicky!

VICKY: What!?

RICK: It's Jessica. I can't see her... She just... disappeared.

VICKY: What...? *(Turning to face Ronnie)* Oh, my God... So's Ronnie.

(RONNIE and JESSICA advance on Charlotte.)

JESSICA: What d'you think we should do with her?

RONNIE: Revenge is a futile emotion, Jessie.

JESSICA: But *very* satisfying.

CHARLOTTE: *(To Vicky and Rick; nervous)* What's going on?

VICKY: We don't know. They've gone.

CHARLOTTE: *(Looking around her; tense)* No... They're still here. I can feel them.

JESSICA: Oh, you're going to feel us alright. Can I go first, Ronnie?

RONNIE: Be my guest.

JESSICA: Right, you cow!

(CHARLOTTE tenses.)

JESSICA: *(Raising her hand to strike. With venom)* Take that! *(She attempts to strike Charlotte but cannot.)* Ronnie... She's blocking me. I can't get near her! *(She tries again.)*

CHARLOTTE: *(Defiant)* Oh, no.... You can't do that. I might not be able to see or hear you, but I know *far* too many tricks for you to hurt me.

RICK: What's going on?

CHARLOTTE: They're trying to exact their revenge.

VICKY: Be careful! They're very powerful.

CHARLOTTE: So am I! I've experienced hundreds of malevolent spirits over the years. I know what to do. They can't hurt *me*!

JESSICA: *(Defeated)* It's no use, Ronnie. You try.

RONNIE: I can't! I can't move!

VICKY: *(Suddenly able to see Ronnie again)* Ronnie!

RICK: *(Suddenly able to see Jessica again)* Jessica!

CHARLOTTE: *(In control)* Ah, I see they've given up! Very wise! I presume they're back with you?

VICKY: Yes.

JESSICA: Ricky. If you care anything for me at all, get her!

RICK: Now hold on a minute! We said we'd help you find the killer. *I'm* no murderer.

VICKY: No. Nor me. This is a job for the Police.

CHARLOTTE: *(Mocking)* The Police!? Hah! What're you going to tell them? They closed the case years ago.

RICK: Well, they can reopen it.

CHARLOTTE: Based on what!? A séance!? You talking to the dead!? It'd be *you* they locked up... not *me*!

VICKY: *(Defeated)* She's right, you know.

CHARLOTTE: Of course I'm right. *(Looking round the room)* I was wrong about you, Ronnie. It would never have worked, would it? I never realised what a child you were. Still, at least I've got you out of my system.

(CHARLOTTE starts to collect her belongings together.)

JESSICA: *(To Rick)* Do something!

RICK: Do something...!? Like what!?

CHARLOTTE: There's nothing you *can* do... You've no evidence. I'm just an eccentric psychic. Nobody takes me seriously. I'll be moving on in the morning... You two - sorry, *four* - will just have to get on as best you can.

JESSICA: *(She has an idea)* Ricky, will you give her a message for me?

RICK: Yes... What?

JESSICA: Ask her if there's any way we *could* harm her.

RICK: Charlotte... Er, Tracy...

CHARLOTTE: Charlotte will do. I've grown quite used to it. What d'you want?

RICK: Jessica wants to know if there's any way they could harm you.

CHARLOTTE: Surely I've already demonstrated that. There's no way on this earth they can harm me.

JESSICA: As I thought... No way... on this earth... *(Sinister)* But we *can* wait... can't we Ronnie?

RONNIE: Oh, yes, Jessie... We can wait.

CHARLOTTE: *(Unconcerned)* What did she say?

RICK: She said they'll be waiting for you. *(After a pause)* You can't live forever!

(CHARLOTTE looks in horror as the message sinks in.)

The CURTAIN closes

The End

Late Of This Address   Lighting & Sound

Furniture & Properties
ACT I Scene 1

ON STAGE:

    Dusty old dresser *(above L)*
Sideboard *(above R)*
    In it: Table knives *(in drawer)*
Table
4 chairs

PERSONAL:

Two old suitcases *(RICK - off R)*
Wristwatch *(RICK)*
Carrier bag from an off licence (VICKY - off R)
    In it: Small bottle of brandy
            Box of matches
Several old books *(CHARLOTTE - off R)*
    including: *"The Spirit World - The Paranormal Explained"*
Large handbag *(CHARLOTTE - off R)*
Flash camera *(CHARLOTTE - round her neck)*
Key *(CHARLOTTE - in her pocket)*

ACT II Scene 1

PERSONAL:

Blanket *(RICK - over him)*
Car keys *(VICKY - off R)*

ACT II Scene 2

PERSONAL:

Wristwatch *(VICKY)*

ACT II Scene 3

PERSONAL:

Wristwatch *(VICKY)*

Late Of This Address   Lighting & Sound

ACT III
ON STAGE:
The room has been significantly tidied.
PERSONAL:
Scarf *(CHARLOTTE)*
Battered folder *(CHARLOTTE)*
    In it: Newspaper cuttings
    including: One with photos of a man and a woman
                  Glossy photograph with names on back
Tray *(VICKY - off L)*
    On it: Three cups of coffee
Glass *(VICKY - on sideboard)*
Lettered cards *(CHARLOTTE - off R)*

Lighting & Sound
ACT I Scene 1

START: Gloomily lit by the light from the window.
CUE 1:   Key in door *(Off R) (P2)*
    After: **CURTAIN UP**
CUE 2: Clunk of a switch *(Off L)* and the room lights come on *(P2)*
    After: **RICK:** Ah!
CUE 3: Sounds of footsteps ascending stairs *(Off L) (P3)*
    After: **RICK:** Don't blow us up, will you?
CUE 4:   Sounds of footsteps descending stairs *(Off L) (P3)*
    After: **VICKY:** ..as if it's been touched for centuries.
CUE 5:   Front door opens and closes *(Off R) (P8)*
    After: **RICK:** See you in five minutes.
CUE 6:   Car starts and leaves *(Off R) (P8)*
    After: **RICK:** Don't forget the brandy!
CUE 7:   Car draws up *(Off R) (P10)*
    After: **JESSICA:** Terrified. I can't think why.... Can you?
CUE 8:   Front door opens *(Off R) (P10)*
    After: **RICK:** I'd better go and help her with the.... er.. matches.

Late Of This Address   **Lighting & Sound**

CUE 9:   Doors opening , footsteps going upstairs *(Off L) (P11)*
     After: **RICK:** What the hell's she up to now? *(Exits L)*
CUE 10:   Key in door, front door opens and closes *(Off R) (P13)*
     After: **VICKY:** No problem. I'm not cold any more.
CUE 11:   Flash photograph *(Taken by Charlotte) (P13)*
     In: **CHARLOTTE:** I might ask *you* the same question.
CUE 12:   Front door slams *(Off R) (P14)*
     After: **VICKY:** Wait...! *(CHARLOTTE exits R)*

ACT I Scene 2

CUE 13:   Footsteps descending stairs *(Off L) (P18)*
     After: **RICK:** All right. I'm sorry. Please come down.
CUE 14:   Muffled pop *(Boiler lighting - off L) (P20)*
     After: **JESSICA:** Easy. *(Snaps her finger)*
CUE 15:   Footsteps going upstairs *(Off L) (P21)*
     After: **RICK:** Right. Ten minutes at the most. *(VICKY exits)*

ACT II Scene 1

CUE 16:   Car draws up, key, door open & slam *(Off R) (P25)*
     After: **CURTAIN UP**

ACT II Scene 2

CUE 17:   Knock on door *(Off R) (P38)*
     After: **RONNIE:** I'm not surprised.
CUE 18:   Louder knock at front door *(Off R) (P38)*
     After: **JESSICA:** No!
CUE 19:   Front door opens & closes *(Off R) (P44)*
     After: **VICKY:** Tomorrow.
CUE 20:   Door L closes behind Vicky *(P46)*
     After: JESSICA *makes a sweeping movement with her arm.*

ACT III

CUE 21:   Knock at door *(Off R) (P58)*
     After: **RICK:** Jessica accepts *your* apology too.
CUE 22:   Front door opens *(Off R) (P58)*
     After: **JESSICA:** He can stay with me.

Late Of This Address   Lighting & Sound

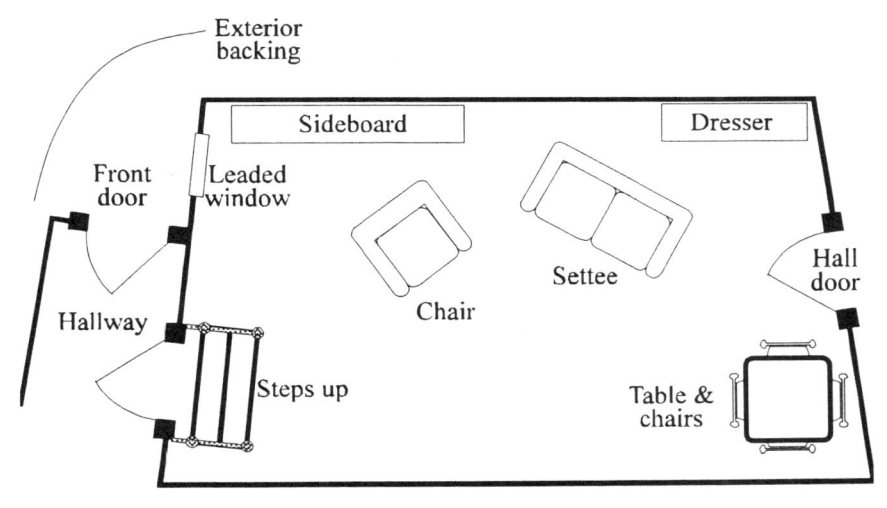

Stage Set with labels: Exterior backing, Front door, Hallway, Leaded window, Sideboard, Chair, Settee, Dresser, Hall door, Steps up, Table & chairs

Stage Set

Note
The above is the minimum required for the play.
It is left to the director to add furniture and
properties to give a realistic "sixties" feel.